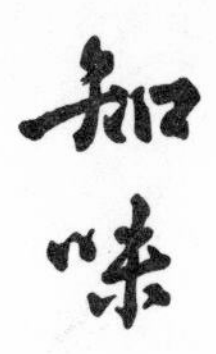

Secrets of Chinese Cooking

By Tsuifeng Lin *and* Hsiangju Lin

With an Essay by Lin Yutang

Drawings by Siu Lan Loh

BONANZA BOOKS · NEW YORK

Second Printing, February, 1970

LIBRARY OF CONGRESS CATALOG CARD NUMBER 60-16720

PRINTED IN THE UNITED STATES OF AMERICA

This edition published by Bonanza Books,
a division of Crown Publishers, Inc.,
by arrangement with Prentice-Hall, Inc.
a b c

Foreword

THIS BOOK IS the result of many years spent away from China, during which we not only had to do our own cooking, but also cook without the ingredients which are common in China and rare abroad. Cooking, which at first had seemed a drudgery, gradually became a joy and an absorbing hobby. Wherever we went, we managed to have simple and nourishing Chinese meals. The technique of Chinese cooking can be applied to almost any ingredients, and though we sometimes longed for some irreplaceable Chinese food, like shark's fins, molded into a perfect hemisphere and served in a lovely sauce, the bulk of our dishes were made from things that could be had at the market. Most of the recipes in this book meet that requirement.

By merely looking through this book the reader should perceive that cooking Chinese food is not a matter of putting in exotic things like edible fungus, but rather that it is a technique. We cook to bring out the texture and flavor of food. The methods of preparing and cooking the ingredients, which are different from those of Western cooking, are designed to bring out the best in a particular cut of meat, a vegetable, or a fish. Chinese cooks have always tried to adapt the method of preparation to the food, and not the food to the method. This is, of course, the logical way to cook, if the individuality of each ingredient is to be emphasized.

So when a cook buys a chicken or a duck, she does not immediately decide on broiling or roasting the bird. First she considers its flavor. If it is a young spring chicken, by all means preserve the fresh tender quality. Cook it with some fresh green vegetables which will blend with the taste of the chicken, or steam it with just a cup of water, a few mushrooms and a slice of ham to make a soup which is light and delightful. In preparing a duck, she takes into account its texture which is apt to be dry and fibrous unless cooked in some liquid till it almost melts in the mouth. If the duck is too fat, she must roast it first to melt the fat before going on with cooking. Add some spinach or Chinese cabbage, for that will cut the grease. The result is, of course, a dish in which all the good qualities of a food have been emphasized, and all the bad ones corrected or toned down. That is what makes the dish so palatable. Chinese cooking, with this attention to flavor and texture, really caters to the gourmet.

From the point of view of the cook, the preparation of Chinese food can be incredibly tedious or simple. This book consists mainly of simple recipes. We have made it so on purpose, because the simple recipes are our favorites (having had to cook ourselves has made them so). To make the book more challenging, we have also put in some fancy ones. By and large, however, this is a collection of recipes from a home kitchen, which we hope will be of some interest and use.

Tsuifeng Lin
Hsiangju Lin

Contents

The Art of Cooking and Dining in Chinese

by Lin Yutang

THE PRESENT BOOK is strictly the record of a family's cooking experience, handed down from a Chinese mother to her daughter, embodying the results of some twenty years of home cooking in America and abroad.

I have seen how the idea of the book was initiated, and how the book grew and came to fruition. In a life of sojourn abroad, a life sweetened with many pleasant memories of home dinners shared with our American friends, I have seen many occasions when our friends asked how such a succulent duck, melting in the mouth yet not greasy, was prepared; how Chinese vegetables could keep their green color and crisp texture; how spinach, sautéed in oil with a sprinkling of chopped garlic, could taste so heavenly; how rice could be cooked so crisp and dry and whole-grained, etc.

I have prided myself on having eaten at the best restaurants in China, but when it comes to telling my friends about the secret of preparing certain dishes, I often have to draw up sharp. "No, no, Y.T. That is not the way." In the end, I feel very humble, though I still stoutly maintain my contribution to the excellent level of my household dinners by acting as a fastidious and discerning critic. The wine-taster still serves a valuable function, even though he does not grow the wine himself.

When the book gradually took form and it came to putting down on paper, not so much the names of the ingredients, as the secret of cutting, drenching, straining them, sometimes freezing them overnight to obtain the requisite crispness, I witnessed another curious process. For six months, off and on in the evenings, when the mother and daughter were not otherwise occupied, I heard the conversations going on in the next room. It was like a party recalling a hunting or fishing trip, or a trip to the Arctic. Any authentic firsthand account of a personal experience is interesting, worth eavesdropping. Not a book was consulted. It was what the psychologists call a total recall.

The mother and daughter dug into their past culinary adventures, with many diversions and corrections, recalling how exactly it was done, and what mistakes there were to avoid. "If you boil a vegetable in cold water, the result may be a delicious soup, but a tasteless vegetable." "After parboiling the vegetable in the water, drench it under the cold water faucet; otherwise the process of heating goes on and the vegetable becomes soft and mushy." Such delightful bits of inside information began to impress me; I was really convinced that the bringing forth of a perfectly cooked dish contained a mystery and a technique worth telling about. When the book was finished, I saw that, succinct as the directions are, every line was the distillation of a lifetime of first-hand experience.

I was later delighted to find out that many of my favorite dishes are to be found in this book—such as seaweed soup and minced perch with black beans—for I was first told that the recipes were to be strictly limited to those calling for ingredients obtainable in American markets. I think all the recipes, conscientiously followed and tested, will open up a field of new flavors at American tables, and add considerably to the culinary delights of many homes.

I need only add that the love of good food, like the enjoyment of good music, is the unmistakable sign of culture. When a man has driven himself to work all day, he has the right to look forward to a delightful supper at home, cooked with respect for the food and for its eater. Admittedly, this is a man's point of view; he does not have to do the cooking himself. I only say that cooking is a high and fine art. The food served at dinner can be an artistic creation, a masterpiece of which the housewife may be justifiably proud, worthy of the admiration of the whole table, or it can be a disaster. It is in such a genial atmosphere of common devotion to good food that the art of cooking is born.

To some, eating is an adventure, a perpetual discovery of new flavors, unknown delights; to others, it is merely a drab necessity of stifling hunger with any solids and fluids. Some eat apologetically, as a regrettable necessity; others, with enthusiasm. First, one should develop respect for cooking as an art, and then the interest and enthusiasm and care

—the willingness to learn and try and fail and try again—the only way in which any art can be cultivated and perfected, with devotion and with patience.

If the subject of good food, tasty food—not calorie contents—were discussed more actively and openly at tables, more commented upon from the pulpits, and editorialized upon in the newspapers, there is no doubt that the matter of cooking and eating would be transformed into a voyage of discoveries and surprises, to the delight of all concerned. Having a good supper becomes then the vision of a hard-working man, as part of a perfect evening, soothing to tired muscles and nerves. Cooking then becomes a domestic function, a mystery like the Greek and Egyptian "mysteries," of which the cook is the high priestess. I quite believe that many souls can be saved and minds edified in the kitchen, and in the kitchen alone. The authors of this book have gone on the very sensible basis of limiting themselves to recipes which are made with ingredients that can be easily obtained at American markets. It is a well self-imposed limitation. They have, however, prepared a special section on more imaginative and exotic dishes which may please more imaginative housewives. The quest for new flavors and new creations is endless. Within limited space, they have given glimpses of what is possible in Chinese cuisine by selected incursions into the domain of the true Chinese gourmet, a territory whose frontiers the average customer of a Sino-American restaurant has not even skirted or suspected.

A whole book might be written on the Chinese art of eating and cooking, the principles involved, the tastes looked for, and the styles of cuisine of the different provinces. It is possible here only to state a few essential points, without expanding them.

Cooking, as the Chinese see it, is a marriage of flavors. *Peng-tiao* means "cook and blend the flavors."

Cooking is also a matter of bringing out the best potential of any given meat or vegetable. A good cook brings out the best that is in a chicken or a duck, in the same way a good educator brings out the hidden talents of a pupil.

If a chicken has been killed, and it is not cooked properly, that chicken has died in vain. If, on the other hand, its true genius has been coerced into self-expression and improved, that chicken will have died at least a worthy death. At least this honor must be done to the chickens, if killing cannot be avoided, in exactly the same way that we honor the war dead.

If it is understood that the essence of Chinese cooking is the blending of flavors, the matching of tastes, the toning down of some aspects of one meat and increasing the piquancy of another then it is easily seen that the *variety* of combinations is practically inexhaustible. That is why Chinese cuisine beats French cuisine in variety.

Style in cooking is like style in writing. Some people overdo it. The best style of cooking remains, for me, not an over-garnished dish which practically smothers the true taste of the particular meat itself, but one which lets the true flavor stand out in all its glory. On occasion, the best food I have tasted is a trout *au bleu,* absolutely fresh and merely boiled in water; the same is true of a barely boiled and freshly killed spring chicken. Only salt is needed, and nothing else.

Poor meat requires an elaborate sauce to cover up its dullness, as a bad writer needs a long-winded vocabulary to cover up his paucity of thought and his lack of fresh ideas.

This type of cooking relying on the true flavor of the meat itself, is best described by the word *delicacy*. It has a clarity of taste like clarity of style in writing. God forbid that such delicate food should be eaten thoughtlessly by busy, important people.

It is against the will of God to taste good food hastily, says a Chinese writer.

Food can be rich in flavor, I grant, like *coq au vin,* or *caneton a l'orange.* Cantonese food is sometimes very rich, and if you like to see a lady all covered up with necklaces and bracelets, go ahead. Peking cuisine has delicacy, on the other hand, and in this respect is Foochow cooking also known. It is more like a young girl from a non-pretentious family who has a natural bloom and gaiety which makes a mockery of all make-up. This is what I would call the orthodox taste.

This purity of taste is best illustrated by that of celery or honeydew melon, which stands out clearly by itself, and does not need blending or intrusion of extraneous flavours.

I have eaten *escargots* in Bourgogne, for instance, freshly prepared, first discovering that French snails do have a taste of their own. Most of the time, however, we are not tasting the *escargots*, but the flavour of sizzling butter and *fines herbes.*

Freshness of food is the soul of cooking. A good cook, proud of her job, spends as much time shopping for food as preparing it in the kitchen.

In China, and in France, a good cook refuses to give food which is not in season and at its best.

Yuan Mei, the poet-gourmet says in his essay on cooking, that half of the art of cooking lies in buying fresh food. Some restaurateurs really insult their customers by serving them spoiled meat with a rich sauce, believing that they are fooling them. If they like to think so, it is their business.

I would say also that a very vital part of any good dinner worthy of the name is the service.

A white table cloth, sparkling glasses and silver service are all part of what contributes to a good dinner. But, more important than anything else, food must be served steaming hot.

Half of the taste of the food is gone when it is allowed to cool at the table. A good food-warmer contributes, vitally, to the enjoyment of good food.

The atrocious custom of cocktails practically makes correct timing of cooked food, be it roast or sautée, impossible. Real guests come to eat—how often this is forgotten—not to nibble at canapes! A New York dinner announced for 7:30 often does not begin till 8:15. How is the cook expected to make good roasts? Such people ought to be given stews. It cannot matter whether a stew is served at 7:30 or at 10:00.

What is needed for the true appreciation of good food is knowledge and accumulated experience. One must have eaten a certain dish, *at its best,* in order to be able to criticize it at all. When one has heard *Othello* spoken by Gielgud or Maurice Evans, then one cannot be satisfied with what is tolerably or fairly good. Or, if one has heard Caruso or Galli-Curci, then one always has a high standard by which to measure the second best.

Therefore, a good cook will insist on what is "just right." What is just right cannot be defined, but is based on what one knows from past experience to be the best.

For each particular dish, one expects a certain particular reaction in the palate, in the same way a music critic expects a certain aria to be sung. A good and well-prepared Chinese *shiangku* (large-sized mushroom) should literally squirt its juices against the cheeks until it fills the whole palate with a voluptuous delight.

The proper appreciation of food is based upon a combination of factors; of teasing the nerve buds of taste in the tongue, the olfactory buds in the nose, the tactile sense of the teeth, and lastly, the visual stimuli of color in the eye.

Food which should be served steaming hot but is allowed to get cold misses half of the full flavor. The importance of the olfactory sense in contributing to the enjoyment of food is often forgotten. It then becomes as tasteless as smoking a cigarette with a stopped-up nose.

Food that should be chewy, or crisp or crunchy depends very much on the type of resistance offered by it to the teeth.

Such variations in consistency are considered of extreme importance in Chinese cooking. In fact, the timing and preparing of food are all directed toward achieving the right consistency—whether it should be crisp, or creamy smooth, or resilient, or luscious, with infinite nuances in its particular kind.

Such nuances are extremely fine and are readily detected by the palate, in the same way that a perfect or a faulty performance at a piano is perceived by a good critic. A complete range of impressions is possible.

How delicate are flavors! This is easily seen in the difference in body and taste and bouquet of wine; the slightest difference is felt and it is that very small difference which is important to the wine connoisseur. And coffee, indifferently prepared or served, can, as everyone knows, taste exactly like dish water.

Some food gains in consistency by being allowed to stand overnight in an icebox, or being flushed under a cold faucet before further treatment.

Sometimes the way a meat is cut, whether in large morsels or in small cubes, affects the taste also. Beef ragout gains immensely by being cut in fairly large morsels because it takes on an opulent quality, and gives a sense of *wallowing* in good food to the tongue. Small slices immediately change the feeling.

A whole world of Chinese flavors is yet unknown and unexplored, particularly the world of Chinese condiments. They play tricks that I know no western condiments can. Soya sauce is pretty well-known; its quality and its possibilities in combination with sugar, wine, vinegar or sesame oil is not yet known.

Oyster sauce, known as *haoyu* (literally "oyster oil"), bids fair to become the next best known Chinese sauce. Oyster sauce is a contradiction: it is and is not an oil; it gives a velvety touch to meat and vegetables *without being greasy.* It does what the corn starch cannot do and has no right to do. It makes the food smooth to the taste without changing its consistency.

There are other very important ingredients which a good Chinese cook cannot do without. Among these are the pickled black beans (*toushi*), essential in preparing sea bass, as the soya bean sauce is essential to fried porgies. They just fit in like a perfect match. This *toushi* appears as tiny black spots in the sauce of "lobster Cantonese style," and is essential to its peculiar flavor. There is wined bean curd (*fuju,* or *toufuju*), tasting like an exotic cheese, but unlike any other flavor known before. There is ginger root which makes all fishy smell magically disappear in preparing shrimp and other seafood. There is sesame oil, very desirable for adding smoothness and aroma to certain kinds of food. There is the seafood sauce (*haishientsiang*) which strengthens the flavor of any food which takes sweet and sour well. There is the *tsatsai,* a salted and piquant preserved vegetable root, which goes well with pork and beef and is dangerously tempting and appetizing. . . . But above all, I place the greatest importance on *toushi,* pickled black beans, one of the greatest creations of Chinese cuisine. It helps digestion to the extent that it takes away all feeling of heaviness after a sumptuous dinner. Given a bit of this crushed black bean, the stomach has a feeling of positive happiness in doing its duties.

There are housewives and housewives. It is perhaps true that some American housewives regard as ideal cooking that which consumes the least time and requires the least thought and skill. It is also true that there are other American housewives to whom cooking is an act of creation, on which much thought and study are spent. These are forever on the quest for the new and the exotic and the unknown, and no one who is so minded ever stops learning. May God bless these imaginative souls! Let their husbands and children be worthy to partake of the food that is finally laid at the table after so much thought and loving care.

The fireplace has gone—as the symbol of the home. Let the dining table be the place where the whole family gathers together and feels human and united once a day. Let it now stand for the symbol of the home.

1

Menus

THE GENERAL IDEA in planning a Chinese dinner is to have the number of dishes equal, or one or two short of, the number of people you are going to feed. That is, for two persons two dishes (for example, a meat and a vegetable) will be sufficient. For four, three or four dishes will do. This rule is applicable to meals for one to eight persons; beyond that number, any meal consisting of eight or more dishes is considered very elaborate.

These dinners are usually beyond the scope of any ordinary cook, and are virtually impossible for the person who has to be hostess as well as cook. The long elaborate dinners are usually delightful, however, and the great variety of the Chinese cuisine prevents the meal from becoming dull. A formal dinner in honor of some guest or a happy occasion might consist of:

4 cold dishes:	Cold Jellied Beef, White Cut Chicken, Cold Lobster, Stuffed Drumsticks
4 hot dishes:	Sautéed Crabmeat, Velvet Chicken, a sweet and sour dish, Shrimp Balls
1st soup:	Steamed Squab, Garnished with Pigeon Eggs
A fowl:	Fried Caraway Chicken
Pork:	Roast Suckling Pig
Duck:	Glazed Duckling
2nd soup:	Turtle Soup
Beef:	Filet of Beef with Mushrooms
A fried dish:	Lobster Claws in Batter
Fish:	Steamed Carp with Bamboo Shoots
Noodles:	Sautéed Noodles
Dessert:	Sweet Almond Soup

If you were invited to a Chinese feast, you might see plates of fruits, nuts and melon seeds on the tables. These are most refreshing in the course of a long dinner. Naturally, one eats only a bite of everything, or two bites if something is particularly good. Bearing this in mind, you would find yourself eating:

Hors d'oeuvres:	Preserved Eggs, Chicken Wings Stuffed with Ham, Butterfly Shrimp, Diced Pork Sautéed with Walnuts
Entrée:	Braised Shark's Fins
Soup:	Woodcock Soup
Duck:	Duck Stuffed with Glutinous Rice, Lotus Seeds and Dates
Pork:	Ham Stewed with Chestnuts
A vegetarian dish:	Bean Curd, Bamboo Shoots Mixed with Greens
Fowl:	Whole Bird's Nest in Chicken
A fried dish:	Fried Squab
Vegetable:	Mustard Greens with Meat Sauce Braised Mushrooms
A fish:	Fried Pomfret with Pungent Sauce
Rice:	Fried Rice with Crabmeat
Fruit:	Lichees

The interesting thing about these dinners is that one is served many courses, yet no taste is repeated. This, of course, is what one must aim for in planning menus for one's own meals.

To have variety and to avoid repetition is a proof of one's skill as a cook. It is also the result of good planning. One gets variety by using different methods of cooking, different ingredients, and by cooking these ingredients so that they all taste different.

When we have guests, I usually plan to have one roast or soufflé, a stew and a soup ready at the back of the stove, something steamed and kept warm on a double boiler, a fried dish and then a dish that is to be sautéed at the last minute

—usually a vegetable. This plan simplifies the problem of serving as everything is ready when needed. From the diner's point of view it is also good because various methods of cooking produce different qualities and textures.

Secondly, one varies the ingredients. This procedure is easily seen in Western dinners, which usually consist of a meat, a fish, vegetables, etc. For interest one can include something unusual and delicious like squid or sautéed kidneys or abalone. Then one must cook these ingredients so that each dish is pleasingly different from its neighbor. It should contrast but not conflict with it. It would be horrible, I think, to be served a sweet and sour dish immediately following something highly flavored like Aniseed Beef. A light, refreshing combination like cucumbers cooked with shrimp would be better. It is comforting to note, however, that most Chinese dishes blend with one another surprisingly well, even though they would never go with one another if cooked in the Western style.

The number of dishes one must prepare is, I repeat, highly variable. Experience has shown me that beyond six dishes one gets diminishing returns. Americans seem to prefer only two or three dishes. They do not like to cope with four or five different flavors at a time. This preference saves a great deal of work and makes for a well-balanced meal.

This is probably the sensible course to take for a woman who is busy with housework and other affairs. The minimum number of courses to make would be two, a meat and a vegetable, or a meat-vegetable dish and a fish, *besides rice.* It should be understood that rice is served with all fish, meat and vegetable dishes. Each person therefore is allowed two portions.

On this basis we have given the approximate number of portions each recipe provides, to make menu planning easier. Following each heading is a number in parentheses; this number denotes the number of portions. When making up the menu, choose the dishes you want and add up the number of portions each dish provides. The total should be *twice* the number you cook for. That is, if you cook for two, provide four portions; for four, eight portions; for eight, sixteen portions. This will provide you with an accurate estimate of the amount of food to be prepared. When the food is served, of course, the Chinese way is to eat as much or as little of each dish as one wants.

Sample Menus

For 2	Fresh Scallops	(2)	
	Sautéed Okra and Tomatoes	(2)	
	Rice		
		4	portions
	Beef with Celery	(2)	
	Steamed Lobster	(2)	
	Rice		
		4	portions
For 4	Shad Roe	(3)	
	Chicken Curry	(3)	
	Lettuce and Watercress	(2)	
	Rice		
		8	portions
For 4	Barbecued Spareribs	(4)	
	Eggplant, Tomatoes, and Bacon	(4)	
	Rice		
		8	portions

Butterfly Shrimps	(3)	
Chicken in Jelly	(4)	
Chinese Cabbage	(2)	
Rice		
	9	portions

For 6

Crabmeat Scrambled with Eggs	(3)	
Aniseed Beef	(5)	
Sautéed Kidneys	(2)	
Stuffed Eggplant	(2)	
Rice		
	12	portions

Shrimp Balls	(4)	
Steak Cubes	(4)	
Minced Squab, Variation 1	(2)	
Steamed Eggs	(2)	
Sautéed Watercress	(2)	
Rice		
	14	portions

White Cut Chicken	(4)	
Pork Balls with Chinese Cabbage	(4)	
Beef with Asparagus Tips	(2)	
Lobster Cantonese Style	(2)	
Sautéed Spinach	(2)	
Rice		
	14	portions

Oyster Pancakes	(3)	
Duck with Chinese Cabbage	(4)	
Beef Stewed with Soy Sauce	(5)	
Rice		
	12	portions

Soup is optional, as in Western meals. If soup is included, the meal will be more substantial. It may be served at the beginning, middle or end of the meal.

In a simple family dinner all the courses are served simultaneously. In a more formal dinner, the dishes appear one by one, so that each receives all the attention of the diners. (This of course is possible only with a cook in the kitchen.)

Rice is served in bowls at the same time as the main dishes, except at formal dinners, where it comes at the end. Dessert is usually omitted, but we often serve fresh fruit or candied ginger, followed by tea or coffee.

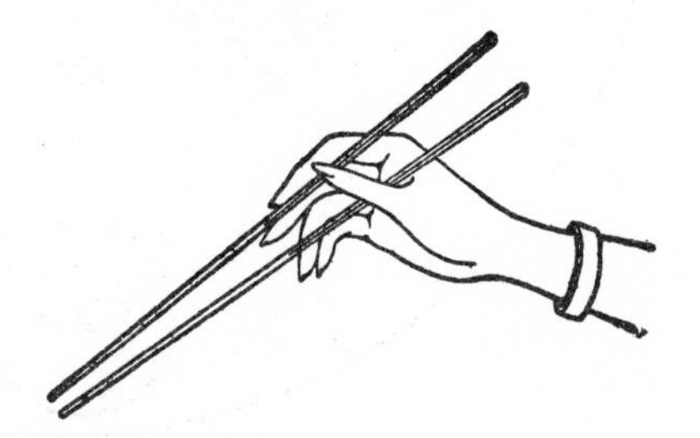

2

Notes

CHOPSTICKS ARE USED by holding them in the right hand, round end down, square end up. Hold the sticks at the middle. The two sticks must be even, or you will not be able to pick things up. The first stick lies between the tips of the first and second fingers; the other stick between the tips of

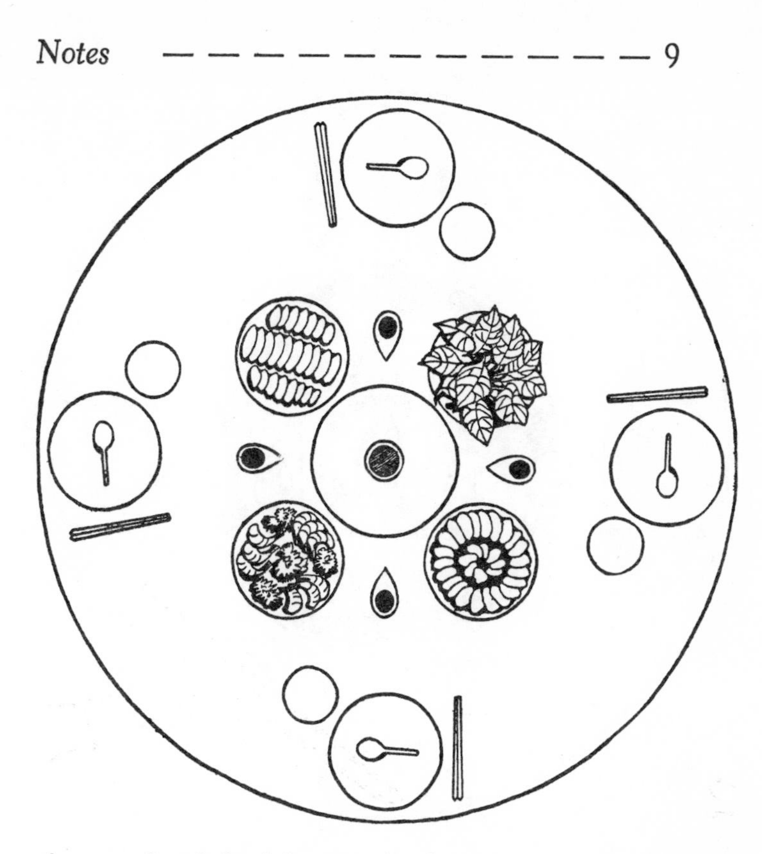

the second and third fingers; the thumb rests against the first stick. The hand is relaxed and in a half open position. By moving the first and second fingers away from the third and fourth fingers, while keeping the thumb resting lightly on the first stick, the first stick is made to move. The second stick is not supposed to move at all. Things are picked up by being held between the two sticks.

Because the Chinese way is to place all the dishes in the middle of the table, and for each person to help himself, a round table is most desirable and convenient. A fairly large lazy Susan, placed in the center, is very useful for holding

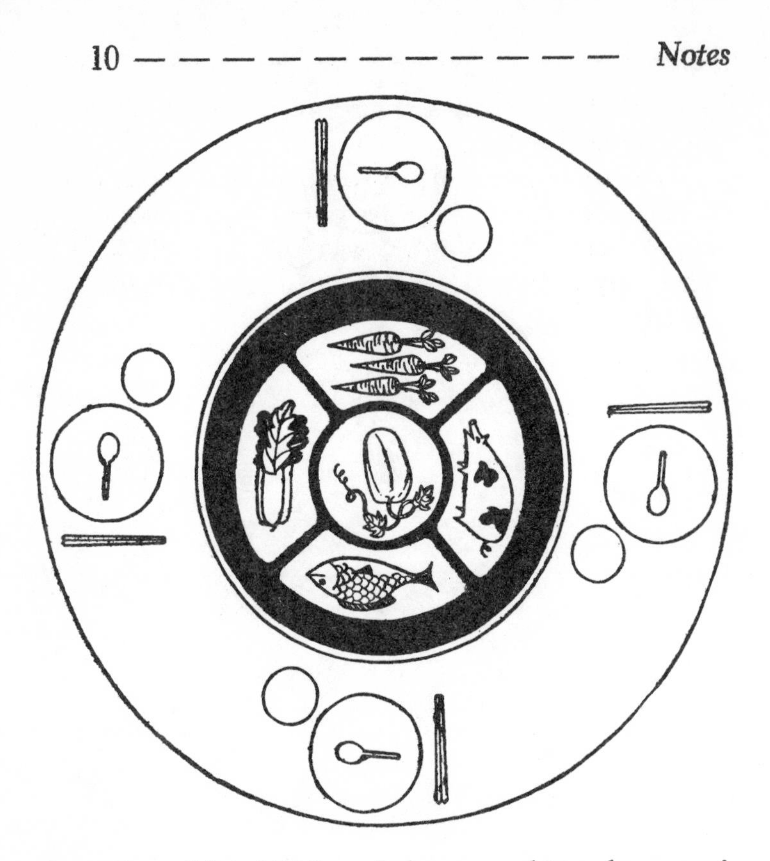

the various dishes. Neither of these two things, however, is absolutely necessary.

Each place is set with a plate; chopsticks to the right, and spoon above the plate. If soup is served at the table, place a soup bowl (smaller than the rice bowl) to the left. Rice is always served in bowls since it stays hot longer that way. In a family dinner, the rice comes with the main dishes; in a more elaborate dinner, where the courses follow one another, rice comes at the end.

Use a spoon for soups, but chopsticks for any noodles or rice. Rice is much more readily picked up by chopsticks if it is in a bowl rather than on a plate, since it is difficult to chase things around a plate.

Soup may be served at the same time as the other courses. It need not be taken right away, and can be placed to one side to cool, to be had in the course of the meal. Wine and liquor may be served during the meal. Tea usually comes at the end.

3
Soups

Here are a variety of soups to choose from. Most of them call for inexpensive ingredients and are easy to prepare.

You may use canned consommé or broth as a base for many of these soups; these take very little time to cook, and as long as other ingredients are added, the taste of the canned soups will not become tiresome.

Note that the simplest ingredients will often yield the finest soups: watercress cooked in chicken broth, for instance, is light and refreshing; while turnips added to beef broth gives it a rich fragrance. Do not hesitate to add thinly sliced bamboo shoots, mushrooms, a few diced shrimps, a stalk of scallion finely chopped, or few slices of ham to your soup. These ingredients will vary the flavor. If your soup is flat, add a few slices of fresh pork and some monosodium glutamate (see page 135), soy sauce and a little pepper. The pork will improve the flavor considerably.

The addition of half a teaspoon or so of brandy to each cup of soup before serving is desirable; this does not apply to vegetable soups, but chicken, beef and pig's knuckle soup all taste better with the brandy.

Remember that in making soup one is trying to extract flavors from the solid ingredients. Slow cooking is desirable in the case of fish or meat. Do not hurry; allow the liquid to simmer and bring out the flavors that are in the meat and bone. Always start the water and the meat or fish at the same temperature; thus both will be heated at the same rate, and the juices are able to flow out of the ingredients. In contrast to slow cooking in making soups, note that ingredients that should have their juices sealed in are quickly broiled, sautéed or fried.

The second rule to follow in making a meat or fish soup (or any soup for that matter) is to use a small quantity of water in proportion to the other ingredients. Do not sacrifice flavor to quantity. Avoid diluting the flavor of the soup too much; otherwise the soup will be tasteless. A three-to-four-pound soup chicken should be cooked in not more than six cups of water. However, if the soup is to be used as stock, it may be diluted a little more.

In general a soup should contrast with the foods that follow or precede it. In Chinese banquets one is often served a creamy soup at the beginning of the meal, and a light refreshing vegetable soup at the end. The richer soup is followed by something fairly light, like sea food; and the vegetable soup acts to cut down any oily taste in the mouth, in much the same way fine tea acts. This is a good rule to apply. Precede a heavy meal with a light soup or broth, and a light supper with a rich soup, so that the different courses will complement each other.

CHICKEN SOUP (4)

Clean

1 (3-to-4 lb.) soup chicken

Place it in

1 to 1½ quarts cold water
1½ teaspoons salt
1 white onion, or a few slices fresh ginger

Simmer covered for two hours.

The secret of good chicken soup is simply this: the less water you use, the better the soup. The proportions given will make you a good soup, but those indicated under Steamed Chicken Soup (see next recipe) yield even better results.

STEAMED CHICKEN SOUP (2)

Clean

1 (1½-lb.) spring chicken

Place it in a Pyrex bowl with

2 medium-sized slices ham
6 medium-sized mushrooms (preferably Chinese)
2 cups cold water
½ teaspoon salt

Place the bowl in a pan of water and cover closely. A double boiler may be used in place of the bowl and pan. Steam for at least 2 hours. When the chicken is done the skin on the drumsticks will pull away from the bone. Since this broth is made with a spring chicken, the meat will be tender. Serve the chicken and the soup together, adding

1 tablespoon brandy

to the soup just before serving.

This makes a very concentrated, nourishing soup. Use only the best ingredients. Do not use ordinary ham; use smoked or fine cured ham, or Chinese ham if possible.

HAM AND CABBAGE SOUP (4)

Grate

1 small head of cabbage

and place it in

1½ quarts boiling water
1 tablespoon salad oil
salt and pepper, to taste

Add

1 ham bone

Simmer covered until the cabbage is tender (about 30 minutes). Remove the bone. Add

½ cup or more ham, cut in slivers

Re-heat for a few minutes.

Cabbage seems to benefit from being cooked with a salty meat such as corned beef or ham. This soup should be cooked until the cabbage is barely soft. It is a hearty and soothing soup, with the flavors of the meat and the vegetable complementing each other.

POTATO AND CORN SOUP (4)

Peel and grate

2 large potatoes

Add

1 quart boiling water
½ teaspoon salt

Cook covered until the potatoes are very soft. Add and heat

1 small can creamed corn

For variety, you may place

½ teaspoon chopped ham
¼ teaspoon chopped parsley

on top of each serving, to garnish the soup

CHINESE CABBAGE SOUP (5)

Cut crosswise into 1½-inch sections

1 medium-sized stalk Chinese cabbage

Heat to boiling

1½ quarts canned chicken broth, or meat stock

Add the cabbage, simmer for 15 to 20 minutes. Season with

salt to taste
1 tablespoon chopped ham

Chinese cabbage, sometimes called celery cabbage in American stores, is sweet and naturally tender; hence very little need be done to make it into a good soup.

CHICKEN SOUP WITH CREAMED CORN (4)

Heat to a boil

3 cans chicken broth

or

1 quart chicken stock

Add and mix

1 small can creamed corn
salt and pepper to taste

If chicken stock is used, you may save the breast meat of the chicken; shred the meat and add it to the soup.

Variation I

Add to the soup a few minutes before serving

½ to 1 cup crabmeat, cooked and flaked

Do not overcook the crabmeat or the flavor will be partially destroyed. This makes a very fancy soup.

Variation II

Add to each serving of soup

½ teaspoon chopped ham
¼ teaspoon chopped parsley

Sprinkle these ingredients on top of the soup to improve its appearance and taste.

This soup is delicious, sweet with corn, and rich with chicken stock. Its creamy consistency and golden color make it a joy to eat. And it is very simple to make, especially if you are using canned soups.

EEL SOUP (4)

Wash and clean

1 (1½-lb.) eel

Leave the skin on and chop it up into 2-inch pieces. Place it in

1 quart cold water
¾ teaspoon salt
¼ teaspoon pepper

Bring the liquid to a boil and simmer covered for 40 minutes. Remove the pieces of fish, bone them, and return them to the soup. Re-heat and just before serving add to each cup

1 teaspoon brandy, or sherry

This is a superb soup. In appearance it is like a consommé, but it is far richer than a plain clear soup, and should be followed by something fairly light. It is very simple to make and its flavor is unique. Note that the skin is left on, contrary to the French method of preparing eel. This gives the soup a slightly oily quality and adds immeasurably to its fragrance.

TURNIP SOUP (4)

Cut into chunks

1 lb. shank beef
2 white onions

Place these in

1 quart cold water
1 teaspoon salt
pepper

Simmer covered for 1½ hours.

Peel, wash and cut into chunks (or make balls using a baller)

1 lb turnips

Add the turnips to the beef broth and simmer for ½ hour more, or until tender.

This is a delicious soup which requires no skill on the part of its maker. The result is one of the most delicately flavored of soups. The addition of bones to the stock will improve its flavor.

TURNIP SOUP WITH CANNED CHICKEN BROTH (4)

Peel, wash and cut into chunks

1 lb. turnips

Place them in

1 quart canned chicken broth
1 teaspoon monosodium glutamate
salt and pepper to taste

Bring to a boil and simmer for about ½ hour.

This soup is simple and cheap.

OX TAIL SOUP (4)

Chop into 2-inch pieces

2 ox tails
2 stalks celery

Peel

4 white onions

Place the ingredients in

1¼ quarts cold water
1½ teaspoons salt
pepper

Bring to a boil and simmer covered for about 2 hours.
Peel

2 large or 3 medium-sized tomatoes

Cut them up into quarters. Add them to the soup and simmer for ½ hour or more.

Here is an excellent soup made with cheap ingredients. The meat on ox tails is finely textured like that of chicken wings. Both these foods are really delicacies if properly cooked.

BEEF SOUP (5)

Cut into 1½-inch cubes

1½ lbs. shank beef

You may add any bones containing marrow to the soup. Combine the beef with

1 to 1½ quarts cold water
2 white onions
2 stalks celery
2 carrots

1 teaspoon salt
pepper

Simmer covered for 1½ hours. Remove the vegetables and meat by passing the soup through a sieve.

The less water you use, the richer the soup will be. Leftover liquid may be reserved for stock.

VEGETABLE SOUP (4)

Peel and slice very thin

1 potato
3 carrots

Chop fine

¼ head cabbage
3 stalks celery
2 white onions

Place these in

1 quart water
½ teaspoon salt
1 teaspoon monosodium glutamate (optional)

Bring to a boil, then simmer covered for at least 1 hour. Pass the soup through a sieve. Before serving place a few drops of vegetable oil on each serving.

WATERCRESS SOUP (4)

Wash

2 cups watercress

If the stems are tough cut them off. Cut into thin slivers

1/3 cup lean pork

Bring to a boil

1 quart meat stock, or substitute

Place the meat in the hot liquid and simmer for about 10 minutes. Add the watercress and boil for 3 minutes. Do not cover the pot or the watercress will turn yellow.

Poach to medium softness

1 egg

and place it on top of the watercress just before serving. When serving the soup, prick the egg to let yolk run out; this will give the soup a nice mild quality, very soothing to the stomach. If you are serving this in the American way, you could poach an egg for each person. Do not allow the yolk to become too hard.

This is one of our favorites. Very easy to make; the only trick is to stop cooking the watercress when it has turned dark green. A fresh-tasting, delightfully clear soup.

FISH SOUP (2)

Boil for a few minutes

3 cups water
3 bay leaves
1 small white onion
1 stalk scallion, chopped
½ teaspoon salt
pepper

Clean

1 pike, or 2 trout

Gently place the fish in the boiling liquid. Cover. Heat over moderate flame until the fish is done (about 10 minutes). Remove the fish and bone. This should be easy if the fish is done. Place a piece of fish on each soup plate. Add

1 tablespoon sherry

to the soup and ladle the boiling soup over the fish.

Be sure to buy fresh fish. Leftover liquid may be reserved for stock.

CUCUMBER SOUP (4)

Cut into thin slices

½ cup lean pork, or ham

Peel and remove the seeds from

2 cucumbers

Cut them crosswise into slices ¼-inch thick.

Bring to a boil

1 quart water
1 teaspoon monosodium glutamate
salt to taste

or

1 quart meat stock

Place the meat and cucumbers in the boiling liquid, cover and simmer for 10 minutes, or until the cucumbers are tender. Stir in

2 eggs, well beaten

A light soup, fine to serve in the summer.

PIG'S KNUCKLE SOUP (6)

Scrub

2 pig's feet
2 upper joints

Place them in

1¾-to-2 quarts water
1 yellow onion, or 4 slices fresh ginger
2 bay leaves
1 teaspoon salt

Simmer for at least 2 hours. The joints should separate easily when done, and the meat should pull away from the bone. Remove the excess fat. Just before serving, flavor with

1 tablespoon soy sauce
2 tablespoons sherry, whiskey, or brandy

A hearty soup; when served with noodles consider it a main dish. Be sure to cook the knuckles until very tender.

ZUCCHINI SOUP (4)

Wash

2 medium-sized zucchini

If the skin seems tough, peel the zucchini. Do not peel young zucchini. Cut the vegetable into ¼-inch rounds.

Heat to a boil

1 quart meat stock, or chicken broth
salt to taste

Add the zucchini and cook for 5 minutes.

Zucchini is gaining popularity in America, as it is quite versatile and flavorful. Try making soup with it. Like all melons, it makes good soup and has that delicate, sweet and tender taste which a vegetable soup should have.

TOMATO SOUP (4)

Peel and cut into wedges

4 medium-sized tomatoes

Slice

1 small white onion

Place the onion and tomatoes in

3 cups cold water
½ teaspoon salt
1 teaspoon monosodium glutamate

Bring to a boil and then simmer for about 10 minutes, until the tomatoes are very soft. When ready to serve, beat

2 eggs

Stir the egg into the boiling soup to make egg drops.

Very quickly made. This is an easy recipe for beginners. When one of my daughters was learning to cook she often treated us to this.

To peel tomatoes, insert a fork into the tomato and hold directly over a gas flame, turning frequently. The skins will then slip off easily.

STOCK MADE FROM SPARERIBS (6)

Bring to a boil, then simmer covered for about 1½ hours

1½ quarts water
1½ lbs. spareribs

2 white onions
2 stalks celery
1½ teaspoons salt

The soup is done when the meat pulls away easily from the bone. Strain. The ribs and vegetables may be discarded. This soup may be used as a base for other soups.

EMERGENCY STOCK (4)

Flavor

3 cups water

with

1 teaspoon monosodium glutamate
pepper
½ teaspoon salt, or 1 tablespoon soy sauce

This is acceptable as a base for soups.

CHAFING DISH (6)

This is a complete meal in itself. The table (preferably a round one) is set with the chafing dish in the center. Plates of raw vegetables, meat, fish, sauces surround the dish. Each place should be set with a plate, a bowl, a spoon and a pair of wooden chopsticks or a fork.

The chafing dish holds a pot of boiling soup. Each person cooks what he will eat by placing it in the hot liquid. In a short while the slice of fish or meat is done. Withdraw the food as soon as it is cooked, dip it into a sauce of your own making and eat it immediately. A delightful way of eating!

Do not make the mistake of putting in too many pieces to

be cooked at one time, nor should you be too hungry, because this is a dish to be eaten at a leisurely pace.

Slice each of the following as thin as possible (a friend of ours has her butcher deep-freeze the meat and slice it on his machine to make the meat paper thin) and arrange each on a separate plate

- ½ lb. boneless lean pork
- ½ lb. liver
- ¾ lb. boned chicken
- 1 lb. shelled fresh shrimp

Wash and thoroughly drain

- 2 cups spinach
- 2 cups lettuce
- 2 cups Chinese cabbage, cut into ½-inch sections
- 1 cup watercress, tough stems cut off

Arrange the vegetables in large shallow bowls. Also place on the table a bowl of

- 12 unbroken raw eggs

Heat first and then place in chafing dish over flame

- 2 quarts meat stock, canned chicken broth, or emergency stock

Add

- 1 tablespoon chopped scallions or parsley, or 1 teaspoon slivered ginger

Keep the broth bubbling all the time. The flavor of the soup improves as the meal progresses owing to all the things that are cooked in it. People who really know how to enjoy this dish wait until everyone else has finished. Then they poach the eggs in the soup, and have the eggs served in the soup.

The following sauces are mixed according to individual taste. Arrange the dishes of the following sauces around the chafing dish

soy sauce (about 1/4 cup)
Oyster Sauce (about 1/4 cup)
vinegar (about 1/4 cup)
1/4 cup peanut butter softened with 2 tablespoons salad oil
1/8 cup sesame seed oil
1/8 cup Hot Sauce

These sauces are explained in the sections on Condiments and Sauces (see page 132).

SWEET PEANUT SOUP (4)

Use only fresh (untoasted) peanuts. Blanch

1 cup peanuts

Place them in

3 cups *lukewarm* water
1 teaspoon baking soda

Cook covered slowly over low heat for at least 1½ hours. Sweeten the soup with

4 tablespoons or more brown sugar

Both this soup and the following one are sweet and are served as a last course in Chinese dinners.

SWEET ALMOND SOUP (3)

Heat

3 cups milk
½ cup sugar

Thicken the milk with

3 tablespoons corn starch dissolved in ½ cup cold water

Stir the starch into the milk and mix until smooth and hot. Add

4 teaspoons almond extract

Heat and serve immediately.

Served hot at the end of a meal, this soup is sweet and soothing to the stomach.

4
Sea Food

JOSEPH WECHSBERG in *Blue Trout and Black Truffles* speaks of a friend who prepared bouillabaisse in the following manner: After catching the fish, he literally dashed back to his kitchen where he set a pot of water boiling. He sorted the fish into two groups, those which would cook rapidly and those which would take longer to cook. The latter he placed in the water first, then when these fish were about done, he added the remainder. I have no doubt that he made a very excellent bouillabaisse.

This little story illustrates two points about cooking sea food. The first is that one should buy the freshest fish possible. Choose one which is clear-eyed and has red gills. The second is that when cooking fish, one should note its texture. Salmon, mackerel, tuna and their like are coarse-textured; hence they take longer to cook than flounder, sole, trout and carp.

Prepare fish by any one of the recipes given in this section; when the fish is done the eyes will protrude, and the flesh will leave the bone easily. When this stage is reached, stop cooking the fish and serve it immediately. Time your courses so that the sea food will not have to be kept over more than ten minutes.

In cooking fish remember to keep the flesh moist and tender; overcooked fish tends to be dry, fibrous and tasteless. Steaming is an excellent way of preparing sea food, because the flesh is kept moist and the temperature is moderate. Baking a fish will dry it out unless it is done in some liquid medium.

In general it is unwise to combine a delicately flavored fish with a highly seasoned sauce. The sauce will "drown out" the flavor of the fish. Use mushrooms, bean curd, eggs and vegetables freely with sole, carp, etc. Save pork, garlic and other highly flavored ingredients for rich meats such as lobster and shrimp. Often it will be unnecessary to add more than a little salt, monosodium glutamate, sherry and parsley to make a dish tasteful. A fresh fish is usually all that is needed to make a delicious soup or main dish.

FRESH SCALLOPS (2)

Wash and wipe dry, and cut into ¼-inch rounds

1 lb. fresh scallops

Slice

1 yellow onion

Brown the onion in

2 tablespoons oil

When the skillet is very hot, add the scallops and stir immediately. Maintain high heat. Sprinkle with

½ teaspoon salt
¼ teaspoon or more black pepper

After the scallops have been sautéed for about 3 minutes, add

1 tablespoon sherry

Permit the alcohol to evaporate. Do not cover the skillet, or the scallops will lose their juice. Sauté for 8 to 10 minutes altogether.

In Chinese cooking most ingredients are quickly sautéed until they are barely *done; at this point one removes them quickly from the heat and serves the dish immediately. Generally the flavor of the original, uncooked food is still present, and this flavor is what cooks try to preserve and enhance.*

Sea food, it seems, benefits particularly from this type of preparation. What we enjoy in sea food is the light, delightfully fresh taste, completely free from oiliness; also the yielding, flaky texture of fish in general.

Scallops are delicately and uniquely flavored; sherry seems to bring out this flavor. When properly cooked their texture is pleasant and their taste is moist. Never deep-fry scallops until they are dry and fibrous. Sauté them quickly in a very

hot skillet with a little oil, sprinkle with black pepper and add a little sherry. Quickly remove them and serve.

SQUID IN TOMATO SAUCE (2)

Slit down the length of their bodies

4 squid

Remove the jelly-like material and cut off the tentacles, if desired. With a sharp knife slash the squid lightly on one side, making diamond patterns. Cut each squid into three or four pieces. Wash the pieces and dry them with a paper towel. (Preparing squid in this fashion before cooking will give good results; the squid must be relatively dry for quick sautéing, and slashing the pieces produces a greater surface area which permits quick cooking.)

Peel and cut into thin slices

3 tomatoes

Crush

2 cloves garlic

Heat in a skillet

1 tablespoon butter

Brown the garlic and remove the cloves from the skillet. Add the tomatoes and sauté them lightly with

¼ teaspoon salt

When the tomatoes are very soft mix in

½ teaspoon Hot Sauce, or Tabasco
1 teaspoon cognac, or sherry

Stir until the sauce is smooth; then pour the sauce into a bowl and set aside. Sauté the squid in a very hot skillet with

1 tablespoon butter

When the pieces begin to curl add

1 tablespoon cognac

Blaze the mixture to permit the alcohol to evaporate. Place the squid immediately in a shallow baking dish. Pour the tomato sauce over the squid and broil quickly to heat the dish through. The sauce should be bubbling hot when it comes to the table.

This dish is copied from a dish we had at St. Jean-de-Luz, in France. We do not think the copy is quite so successful as the original, but it is quite good nevertheless.

This dish is interesting and excellent for several reasons. The first is that the quick heat used in sautéing and broiling the squid gives it a marvelous texture, resilient but not tough. The second is that the sauce is a perfect complement to the flavor of the squid. Like all perfect combinations one cannot alter any part without detracting from the whole.

SAUTÉED SQUID (2)

Slit down the length of their bodies

4 squid

Remove the jelly. Slash the squid diagonally in both directions, making diamond patterns. Cut the squid into pieces 1 inch by 2 inches. Wash, then dry with paper towel. Wash and chop coarsely

2 stalks celery

Heat in a skillet

1½ tablespoons oil

When the oil is extremely hot add the squid; stir immediately and constantly. When the pieces begin to curl add

1 tablespoon sherry

Maintain high heat. Remove the squid, leaving the juices in the pan. Add the celery to the pan and sauté for 2 or 3 minutes, then return the squid to the skillet. Mix over high heat. Season with

¼ teaspoon salt
pepper

Serve immediately.

Highly recommended. The celery enhances the fresh flavor of the squid. Be sure to have the skillet as hot as possible, and do not let this dish stand for more than a few minutes, or the crisp texture of the squid will be destroyed. Do not add salt till the very last, or the squid will be tough.

OYSTER PANCAKES (3)

Drain and chop coarsely

1½ cups oysters (fresh or frozen; if frozen, thaw completely)

Set aside

¼ cup oyster liquor

Wash and chop fine

5 stalks scallions

Beat

4 eggs
oyster liquor
½ teaspoon salt
¼ teaspoon pepper

Add the scallions and oysters to the egg mixture and mix briefly. Add

4 tablespoons flour
½ teaspoon baking powder

Mix until blended only. Drop the mixture into hot fat from a large spoon and fry until golden brown, turning them once. Serve at once with a sauce made from

6 tablespoons vinegar
3 teaspoons Hot Sauce

Place the above mixture in a little dish.

Eggs, oysters and scallions combined in a fragrant dish native to my home town.

OYSTER AND CLAM SOUFFLÉ (6)

Thaw and heat to the boiling point

1 package frozen oysters
1 package frozen clams

Remove from heat and set aside. Meanwhile, chop

1½ cups scallions

Beat together

5 egg yolks
½ cup milk

Set aside the

5 egg whites

Sauté the scallions in a large skillet for 2 minutes in

⅓ cup salad oil

When the scallions have been sautéed for 2 minutes stir in

6 tablespoons flour

Over low heat, slowly add while stirring

1 cup milk
1½ teaspoons salt
¼ teaspoon pepper

When the mixture is smooth and hot, add the oyster and clam

liquor. There should be about 1 cup of liquor. Stir until smooth over low heat. When the sauce is hot, add the clams and oysters, and heat for about 1 minute.

Remove any fishy odor by adding

1 tablespoon brandy, or sherry

Add the egg yolks in a thin stream, stirring constantly. Stir until the mixture thickens, about 15 minutes. The sauce is thick enough when the pieces of clam and oyster no longer sink to the bottom. Cool and store in the refrigerator.

When ready to make the soufflé, beat the egg whites until stiff, seasoning with

¼ teaspoon salt

Fold the egg whites into the oyster mixture and pour into a deep Pyrex bowl. Bake uncovered for about 1 hour in a moderately hot oven (325° F.). The top should be lightly browned when the soufflé is done.

Soufflés are unknown in Chinese cuisine, but we are including this anyhow because it is so good. When cooking for American friends I sometimes make this, Chicken Stewed with Chestnuts, a sautéed green vegetable and rice. For dessert: melon balls made from cantaloupe, honeydew melon and watermelon, well chilled.

CRABMEAT SCRAMBLED WITH EGGS (2 OR 3)

Flake

½ lb. (about 1 cup) crabmeat

You may use less crabmeat and more eggs, if desired. Beat

4 eggs
½ teaspoon salt

¼ teaspoon pepper
1 tablespoon chopped scallions (optional)

Sauté the crabmeat gently in

1½ tablespoons oil, or butter

When the crabmeat is hot, add some more

oil, or butter (about 2 tablespoons)

When the butter has melted, add the eggs. Turn the heat to high. With a fork draw the solidified egg to the center of the skillet, tilt the skillet and let the uncooked egg run over the pan. Repeat this procedure until most of the egg has set. Serve immediately.

A delicious combination. Easy to make. Never overcook the eggs. Serve them while the eggs are still semi-liquid and partly set.

CRABMEAT SOUFFLÉ (6)

Flake

1 lb. (about 2 cups) crabmeat

Beat together, setting aside the whites

6 egg yolks
½ cup milk

Chop fine and set aside

¼ lb. ham

Chop fine

3 stalks scallions, or 1 small white onion

Sauté the scallions over low heat for 1 minute in

⅓ cup salad oil

While the scallions are still bright green stir in

5 tablespoons flour

When the flour mixture is smooth slowly add

1½ cups milk

Stir constantly over low heat until the mixture is hot. Add the ham and the crabmeat and heat for 1 minute to permit the flavors to blend. Season with

1 teaspoon salt
⅛ teaspoon pepper, or curry

Add if desired

2 teaspoons sherry

When the above ingredients are blended add the egg yolks, pouring in a thin steam with constant stirring. Maintain very low heat and stir for about 10 minutes, to permit the yolks to thicken. When the sauce thickens remove it from heat immediately. Cool.

Beat the egg whites with

¼ teaspoon salt

Fold them into the crabmeat mixture. Bake for about 55 minutes in a moderate oven (325° F.).

The trick here is to use low heat during the mixing of the ingredients, so that the flavor of the crabmeat is not destroyed.

CARP IN CHICKEN FAT (4)

Wash and clean

1 (2½-lb.) carp (with or without roe)
2 stalks scallions or 2 cloves garlic

Cut the scallion into ½-inch pieces, or crush the garlic. Sauté these in

⅓ cup chicken fat

Maintain high heat. Place the carp in the skillet and brown

each side for about 3 minutes. When both sides are brown, pour over the fish

2 tablespoons soy sauce, or 1 teaspoon salt
2 tablespoons sherry

Allow a minute or two for the sherry and soy sauce to penetrate. Then add

¾ cup water

Cook over moderate heat, turning the fish after 10 minutes. Cook the other side 10 minutes.

Carp is noted for the delicate flavoring of its flesh and for its soft texture. When it is cooked in chicken fat, both of these qualities are brought out.

STEAMED FISH (3)

Wash

1 sea bass (about 1½ lbs.)

Do not remove the head, since a whole fish looks better than a decapitated one. Place the fish on a platter which will fit into a larger pan for steaming. Sprinkle the fish with

½ teaspoon chopped fresh ginger, or scallions
1 tablespoon sherry
1 tablespoon soy sauce
1 tablespoon oil

Partly fill pan with water and place wax paper between platter and pan to prevent platter from knocking around (for best results use 6 inch strip, fold in half lengthwise and in half again). Cover the pan and keep the water boiling. Steam for about ½ hour, or until the eye of the fish is white and protrudes.

Fish which are quickly cooked and delicate in texture are suited to this method of preparation. Steaming a fish will keep its skin and flesh moist, at the same time permitting the fish to be cooked in its own juice. The juice of the fish frequently will taste too sharp, and for this reason oil is added to the liquid to counteract its keenness. The soy sauce, scallions, ginger or garlic, of course, all enhance the flavor of the fish.

You may use porgy, sea bass, trout, filet of sole, flounder, or any other finely textured fish.

SOY SAUCE FISH (3)

Clean and wipe dry

1 carp, pike, sea bass, or trout (about 2 lbs.)

Make 1 or 2 diagonal slashes on each side of the fish, for faster cooking.

Heat in a skillet

2 tablespoons oil

Add

2 stalks scallions, or 1 stalk leek, split lengthwise and cut into ½-inch sections

When the skillet is extremely hot add the fish. Cover and brown one side (about 2 minutes). Turn the fish over and brown the other side. Pour out about half the fat. Reduce the heat to moderate.

Add

3 tablespoons soy sauce
3 tablespoons water
1 tablespoon sherry
1 teaspoon brown sugar (optional)

Cover and cook each side 5 minutes. Add a little more water if necessary.

This is a simple and delicious way to prepare fish. The sauce is savory and no trouble to make, since all the ingredients are simply poured over the fish and cooked for a few minutes.

FISH IN CRUST (5)

Wash, dry and split down the back, removing the bones

1 large (about 2 lbs.) sea bass, porgy, bluefish, or sole

Beat until frothy

2 egg whites

Dip the fish in the egg white, then roll it in

flour

Repeat the procedure.

Heat in a skillet

2 tablespoons oil

When extremely hot, fry fish until brown on both sides.

Serve with

lemon wedges and ketchup, mixed with a little Hot Sauce

or

soy sauce

or

Pungent Sauce (see recipe on next page)

An interesting variation on fried fish. The crust protects the fish and prevents it from becoming dry.

FISH WITH PUNGENT SAUCE (3)

Cut into pieces 1 inch by 2 inches

¾ lb. boned pike, or sole

Dip them in the batter given under Phoenix Tail Shrimp (see page 55). Fry them in deep fat and drain on absorbent paper.

Prepare a sauce by heating together

2 tablespoons oil
2 tablespoons vinegar
1½ tablespoons sugar
2 tablespoons water
¼ teaspoon salt
2 tablespoons ketchup

Stir until smooth and bubbling. Add to the sauce

¼ cup carrot slivers
¼ cup thinly sliced tomatoes
¼ cup green pepper strips

Sauté these ingredients for 2 or 3 minutes. Add the fried fish and combine gently. When all the ingredients are heated, remove from heat and serve immediately.

FRIED PORGY (4)

Clean and wipe dry

2 medium-sized porgies

Make 2 diagonal slashes on each side of the fish. This will permit faster cooking.

Heat

2 tablespoons oil

Have the skillet very hot before placing the fish in the pan, or it will stick. Cover. Cook each side about 6 minutes. Turn the fish only once. Drain off the oil and serve the fish with

soy sauce

A simple, good dish for family dinners, which might consist of

Fried Porgy
Beef with Tomatoes *(See page 83)*
Steamed Eggs *(See page 112)*
Rice *(See page 138)*

SAUTÉED PIKE (3)

Bone
    ¾ lb. pike
Cut the pike into slices 2 inches by 1 inch.
Wash and cut into flowerets
    ½ head cauliflower (about 1 cup)
Cut the flowerets into very thin slices.
Wash and slice very thin
    1 cup mushrooms
Cut into 1-inch pieces
    2 stalks scallions
Sauté the cauliflower, mushrooms and scallions in
    2 tablespoons oil
adding
    ½ teaspoon salt, or 1 tablespoon soy sauce
    ½ teaspoon monosodium glutamate
Add the pike, maintaining high heat. Stir until the fish is done (about 10 minutes). If necessary, add
    1 tablespoon water

Vary this dish by substituting other vegetables for the cauliflower, mushrooms and scallions.

FISH BALLS (4)

Skin and bone

1½ lbs. pike

Put the fish through the grinder twice. Place on a board and chop, adding gradually

½ cup cold water
½ cup corn starch

Chop until the mixture becomes a stiff paste. Add to taste

salt
monosodium glutamate

Shape the mixture into balls, and drop them from a teaspoon into a large bowl of cold water. This will prevent the balls from sticking. Cook the balls in rapidly boiling water. When they are cooked they will float to the surface. Remove them, and when they are cool store them in the refrigerator overnight.

Set aside the water in which the balls have been cooked. Season it with

salt to taste
½ teaspoon monosodium glutamate
chopped parsley

Before eating, heat the balls in the boiling liquid and serve them with the broth they were cooked in. There should be enough liquid to cover the balls.

These are best when prepared a day in advance and stored in the refrigerator. This method gives them a resiliency which they would otherwise lack.

MUSHROOMS STUFFED WITH FISH (3)

Wash thoroughly and drain

¾ lb. large mushrooms (use caps only, discarding stems)

Chop together

½ lb. fish filets (sole, flounder, or pike)
a few celery leaves, or some parsley

Mix the fish with

¾ teaspoon salt
1 teaspoon sherry

Fill the mushroom caps with the fish, using a butter knife to make the surface smooth. Spread the mushrooms with

2 slightly beaten egg whites

This will make the fish stick.

Heat in a skillet

3 tablespoons oil

When the oil is fairly hot place the mushrooms, fish side up, in the fat and cover. The mushrooms will absorb the oil. If they become too dry add

2 tablespoons water

Cook the mushrooms for about 8 minutes, or until done. Remove them, leaving the juices behind. Prepare

1½ cups Chinese cabbage, cut into 2-inch sections

Sauté the cabbage in the juices of the mushrooms, using moderate heat. Add

½ tablespoon soy sauce

When the vegetable is barely soft (about 5 minutes), reduce the heat, add the mushrooms and cover to permit the flavors to blend. This should take about 2 minutes. Meanwhile mix together

1 teaspoon monosodium glutamate
1 tablespoon corn starch
¼ cup cold water

Pour this over the cabbage and mushrooms and blend gently, until the mixture is smooth and the starchy taste gone (about 1 minute).

These are rather fun to make. They are useful for parties as waiting does them no harm. Use Chinese mushrooms if available, as these are by far more flavorful. Suggested menu for six:

Chicken Soup with Creamed Corn *(See page 17)*
Mushrooms Stuffed with Fish
Soy Sauce Chicken *(See page 92)*
Beef with Asparagus Tips *(See page 81)*
Fried Pork with Walnuts *(See page 67)*
Rice *(See page 138)*

SWORDFISH IN TOMATO SAUCE (4)

Wash, peel (if desired) and cut into quarters

3 medium-sized tomatoes

Chop

2 stalks scallion

Sauté scallions in

2 tablespoons oil

When the skillet is fairly hot, place in it

1 lb. swordfish

Cover. After 2 minutes, turn the fish over on the other side. Season with

½ teaspoon salt
¼ teaspoon black pepper

Add the tomatoes and reduce the heat. Cook covered for about 10 minutes, until the fish is done.

Swordfish is suitable for this recipe because it is firm and flavorful. The sauce, which is made in the same pan, prevents the fish from becoming too dry.
For a family dinner, to serve three, this recipe and Minced Pork with String Beans *(see page 65)* *will fill the bill.*

SHAD ROE (3)

Clean, dry and dredge with flour
1 lb. shad roe
Wash and chop
2 stalks scallions
Sauté the scallions over moderate heat in
1½ tablespoons oil
Place the roe in the skillet and brown each side. Now add
1½ tablespoons soy sauce
1½ tablespoons sherry

Baste the roe with the sauce, cover the skillet and cook for 10 to 15 minutes, or until done.

Rich, with a mild flavor like the yolk of an egg. For a party of five you could have:
Tomato Soup *(See page 25)*
Shad Roe
Chicken with Cucumbers *(See page 103)*

Broccoli with Beef (See page 77)
Rice Scrambled with Eggs (See page 139)

LOBSTER CANTONESE STYLE (2)

Wash and chop into 2-inch sections, shell and all

2 uncooked lobsters (about 1 lb. each)

Chop fine and set aside

¼ lb. pork

Crush

4 cloves garlic

Brown the garlic in

2 tablespoons oil

Add the pork and sauté for about 3 minutes, seasoning with

1¼ tablespoons soy sauce

Remove the pork but leave the liquid in the skillet. Add the lobster and cook it over high heat, stirring constantly. When the lobster is done (a bright red color), return the pork to the skillet. Mix together and add

2 tablespoons cornstarch
1 cup water

Heat the mixture through. Beat together

2 eggs
3 tablespoons water

Add this to the lobster and cook over low heat, stirring constantly. The egg will form a sauce with the liquid in the skillet; remove from heat while the egg is still in the creamy stage.

Popular in Chinese restaurants, and rightly so. The sauce should be tasty but not rich, creamy but not heavy; the lob-

ster should be succulent and juicy. This is probably one of the best ways ever invented to cook lobster.

STEAMED LOBSTER (2 OR 3)

Wash and split down the back

2 lobsters (1 lb. each)

Have ready a fairly deep dish which will fit into a large pan or skillet. Fill the pan partly with water and place a 6-inch piece of paper folded twice between the pan and the dish to prevent knocking. Arrange the lobster on the plate meat side up, and sprinkle the pieces with about

½ teaspoon salt

Spoon the following ingredients over the lobster in this order

1 tablespoon sherry
2 teaspoons vegetable oil
2 teaspoons finely chopped scallions

Cover the pan and steam for ¾ hour, or until shell is red.

Choose a rich vegetable to go with this, such as Eggplant with Garlic (see page 128).

STUFFED MUSHROOMS WITH PORK AND SHRIMP (3)

Remove the stems from

¾ lb. large mushrooms

Shell and wash

½ lb. shrimp

Grind the shrimp together with

¼ lb. pork
1 stalk celery, or some parsley
½ teaspoon salt
pepper

Fill the mushroom cavities with the pork and shrimp mixture. Heat

3 tablespoons oil

Place the mushrooms in the fat, filled side up. Cover and cook over moderate heat. Season the mushrooms with

2 teaspoons soy sauce, or ½ teaspoon salt

If the mushrooms threaten to burn, reduce the heat and add

2 tablespoons water

About 10 minutes cooking time will be sufficient.

These are delightfully juicy, flavorful morsels. They look pretty garnished with a bit of parsley, are excellent as hors d'oeuvres or in a cold buffet.

SHRIMP WITH CELERY AND ALMONDS (4)

Shell and remove the veins from

1 lb. shrimp

Wash, dry and dice them. Dice

3 stalks celery (about 1 cup)

Chop coarsely

½ cup blanched and toasted almonds

Sauté the shrimp over high heat for about 3 minutes with

1½ tablespoons oil

Season with

salt to taste

½ teaspoon monosodium glutamate
1 teaspoon sherry

Remove the shrimp. Add the celery and almonds to the juice of the shrimp and sauté quickly for about 1 minute. Add to the celery mixture

¼ teaspoon salt

Combine the shrimp with other ingredients and heat well. Do not permit the celery to lose its crispness.

SHRIMP ON TOAST (makes about 40 canapés)

Chop fine or grind together

1 lb. shelled shrimp
1 teaspoon salt
⅛ teaspoon pepper
1 teaspoon sherry
A few leaves celery, or parsley

Add

2 egg whites, well beaten

Cut off the crust from

1 small loaf white bread, thin sliced.

Cut each slice of bread into 4 squares. Spread each square of bread with about ¼ inch of the shrimp mixture. Heat 1 inch oil in a skillet. When the oil is hot place the squares, bread side up, in the fat. Fry the shrimp side for a few minutes, then turn and brown the bread. Drain on absorbent paper. To keep these warm, place them uncovered on a cookie sheet in a slow oven (300° F.). These squares taste best, however, when served immediately.

This is fine with cocktails or as an appetizer.

BOILED SHRIMP (4)

Rinse in cold water

1 lb. shrimp

Drop them into

2 cups boiling water
½ teaspoon salt

Cover and boil for about 4 minutes, or until bright pink. Drain and cool. Shell them and serve with the following sauce.

Sauce

½ teaspoon horseradish, or ½ teaspoon chopped fresh ginger
2 teaspoons sugar
2 teaspoons vinegar
4 tablespoons soy sauce

Stir until dissolved.

SHRIMP WITH GREEN PEPPERS (4)

Shell, clean, wash and drain

1 lb. fresh shrimp

Cut the shrimp into 1-inch pieces and dredge them with

1½ tablespoons corn starch, or flour
salt and pepper to taste

Wash and remove the seeds from

3 green peppers

Quarter them and cut each quarter into 2 or 3 pieces. Sauté the shrimp in

1½ tablespoons oil

Add

1 tablespoon sherry

Mix well. Allow the alcohol to evaporate, then remove the shrimp but leave the liquid in the skillet. The shrimp need not be completely done at this stage. Sauté the peppers in the liquid over high heat, adding a little

salt

to the peppers. Do not cook the peppers for more than 4 or 5 minutes. Add the shrimp and combine.

Green peppers tend to become bitter when overcooked. Serve them while they are still bright green and retain the texture of the raw vegetable.

To serve four, you might have:

Watercress Soup (See page 21)
Shrimp with Green Peppers
Aniseed Beef (See page 79)
Garlic Spinach (See page 126)
Rice (See page 138)

SAUTÉED SHRIMP (3)

Remove the legs and the sand (use small scissors) from

1 lb. shrimp

Rinse and dry them. Heat together in a skillet

2 tablespoons oil
2 tablespoons soy sauce
2 tablespoons brown sugar
2 tablespoons sherry
½ tablespoon vinegar
½ tablespoon chopped fresh ginger (optional)

When the sauce is bubbling add the shrimp. Sauté over high heat for about 5 minutes, covering the skillet. Serve hot or cold.

Unshelled shrimp tend to be more tender than shelled ones because the flesh is protected by the shell during cooking.

This recipe is very simple to make and foolproof. Have this with cocktails, to eat with your fingers.

PHOENIX TAIL SHRIMPS (3)

Very good!

Wash

1 lb. shrimp

Remove all but the tail section of the shell. Split the shrimp halfway down the back and remove the sand. Rinse and dry the shrimp. Prepare the batter by mixing into a paste

1 cup flour
1 teaspoon salt
½ teaspoon pepper
½ cup water

looks funny at this stage, but continue it is good!

When you are ready to use the batter add to it

3 teaspoons baking powder

Hold the shrimp by the tail and dip it in the batter. Fry immediately in moderately hot deep fat until golden brown. Serve at once, or keep the shrimp hot in an oven (300° F.). Do not cover them, or they will become soggy.

Excellent with cocktails. The batter may also be used for fish filets; it makes a very light airy crust which is delicious.

SHRIMP WITH GREEN PEAS (3)

Shell, wash, remove sand and dice

¾ lb. shrimp

Dredge them with

2 teaspoons corn starch, or flour
½ teaspoon salt
½ teaspoon monosodium glutamate
pepper

Sauté the shrimp until half done only in

1½ tablespoons oil

Remove the shrimp, leaving the juice in the skillet. Add

1 box frozen peas

When the peas are almost done (4 to 5 minutes) add the shrimps. Combine. Stir in

1 tablespoon water

Heat for 2-3 minutes more, until shrimp are done.

A very pretty dish. It may be wise to buy small shrimp, which have a finer texture than the larger ones.

SHRIMP BALLS (4)

Shell, remove the sand from

1½ lbs. shrimp

Wash and dry them. Chop the shrimp into a fine paste, adding

½ teaspoon salt
pepper

Beat until stiff

1 egg white

Mix the egg white with the shrimp and drop the balls from a spoon into very hot deep fat. There should be enough fat to permit the balls to float in it. When the balls are golden brown drain them on absorbent paper and serve them immediately, sprinkling them with

nutmeg
lemon juice

Light, puffy and golden brown, these balls should be resilient when you bite into them. They are quite delicious.

CURRIED SHRIMP (4)

Shell and remove the sand from

1½ lbs. shrimp

Wash the shrimp. If they are large, cut them in half. Peel and cut into wedges

3 white onions

Sauté the onions for 3 to 4 minutes in

1½ tablespoons oil
1 teaspoon curry

Add the shrimp and cover, stirring occasionally until done (about 10 minutes). Use moderate heat. Add to the shrimp

¾ cup milk

Thicken the sauce with

1½ tablespoons corn starch dissolved in water

Stir until smooth and serve immediately.

This is especially good served with rice and a crisp salad made with endive, celery, radishes and watercress. Add more or less curry according to your taste.

BUTTERFLY SHRIMP (3)

Shell and remove the sand from

1 lb. shrimp

Rinse and dry them. Cut in half

bacon strips

Wrap a piece of bacon around each shrimp and fasten with a tooth pick. Sprinkle with pepper.

Variation I

Fry the shrimp in deep fat. Drain on absorbent paper and serve with

lemon wedges

Variation II

Sauté the shrimp in

1½ tablespoons oil

When the shrimp are almost done add

½ cup ketchup

Cook the shrimp in this until done and serve very hot.

For two or three persons, serve:

Butterfly Shrimps II
Chicken with Peppers (See page 102)
Rice (See page 138)

SHRIMP WITH CUCUMBERS (3)

Shell and remove the sand from

1 lb. shrimp

Cut the shrimp into bite-size pieces and dredge them with

2 tablespoons corn starch

½ teaspoon salt

pepper

Peel and split in half lengthwise

2 cucumbers

Remove the seeds and cut crosswise into ¼-inch sections. Peel and slice into rings

1 white onion

Sauté the onion for 2 minutes in

2 tablespoons oil

When transparent, add the shrimp and stir constantly. When the shrimp turn pink, add the cucumbers. Cover and reduce to moderately low heat. Stir occasionally and remove from heat when the cucumbers become translucent (about 8 to 10 minutes).

This looks pretty and tastes very fine. Light green and pink in color, these delicate tones are matched by the delicate flavors of the shrimp and cucumber. Be sure to stop cooking this dish when the cucumbers first become translucent.

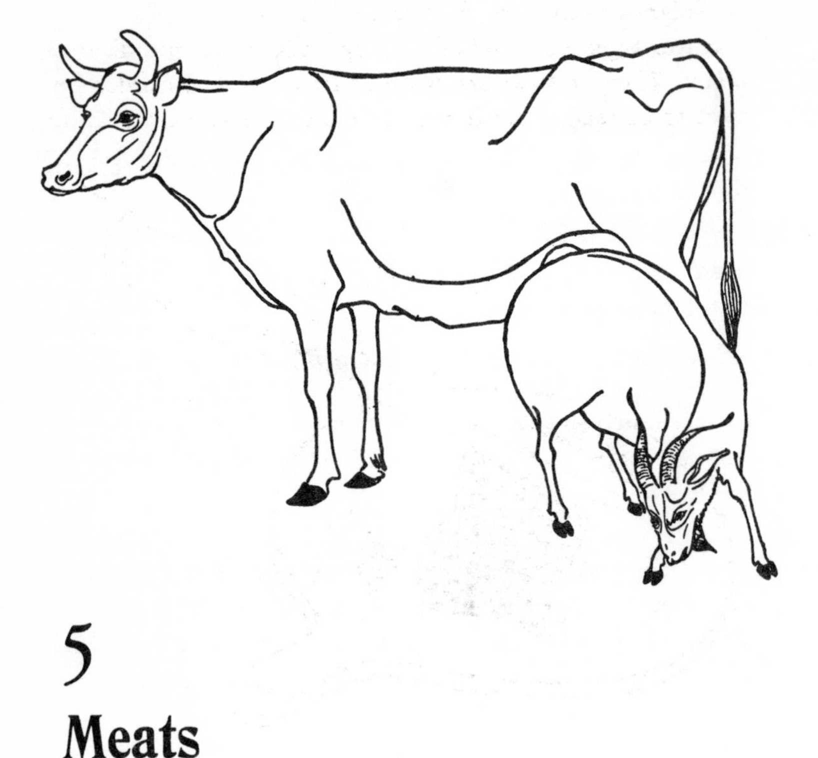

5
Meats

MOST OF THE RECIPES given in this section call for a relatively small amount of meat. This is characteristic of Chinese cooking.

As a rule we seldom serve large chunks of meat like steaks, though we do make roasts. Combined with vegetables or other foods, our meat is cooked in such a fashion as to make a little go a long way. The seasonings and the mode of cooking are all designed to enhance the flavor of the meat.

In our typical method of cooking, meat is cut into slices or slivers. These small pieces permit fast cooking. In order for meat to be tender, cut it across the fibers, holding the knife

perpendicular and diagonal to the grain. *Have all the ingredients ready before starting.*

Heat the skillet with a little oil and add onions or fresh ginger. Brown the onions. Have the skillet very hot before adding the meat. Sauté the slices by stirring lightly and constantly for a few minutes. Maintain high heat while sautéing the meat. Do not add the liquid seasonings such as soy sauce or sherry too early. Cooking meat in watery liquids will toughen it. Add the liquid seasoning only when the meat slices are half done. Permit the slices to absorb some of the liquid, sprinkle with salt, pepper or monosodium glutamate at this time, if required. If other ingredients are to be combined with the meat, remove it when three-quarters done. You will finish cooking it later. Set aside the meat in a dish, leaving any juices in the skillet. Sauté the other ingredients in the juice of the meat. When these are about done, add the partially cooked meat, combine, and cook until all are done. Serve immediately.

This method of cooking permits the blending of flavors without sacrificing the texture of the individual foods.

SLICED LAMB WITH LEEKS (2)

Clean

4 leeks (or 3 cloves garlic, crushed)

Split the leeks down the middle and hold them under the tap. Cut them into 1-inch pieces. Trim

1 lb. lamb

Slice the lamb as thin as possible into pieces 2 inches by 1 inch. Sauté the leeks in

2 tablespoons oil

When the edges of the leeks are brown, add the lamb and stir constantly. Maintain high heat. Add at the very last

¾ teaspoon salt
1 teaspoon monosodium glutamate

This dish should take no more than 5 minutes to cook, if the skillet is hot enough. Serve immediately. This is a dish of northern China. It is especially good eaten piping hot on a soft bun. Serve wine with it.

MINCED PORK (3)

Meat is more tender when chopped by hand than when ground by a machine. Chop (or put through a meat grinder)

1½ lbs. lean pork
½ cup celery
1 stalk scallion

When the meat is finely ground add

¾ teaspoon salt, or 1 tablespoon soy sauce

Sauté the meat in a very hot skillet with

1 tablespoon oil

Stir constantly. After 2 or 3 minutes add

1 tablespoon sherry, or whiskey

Stir and mix until the meat is brown and the liquid has been absorbed, and serve immediately. The pork should still be somewhat moist.

With pork serve

whole lettuce leaves, washed and drained

A small portion of the pork is placed on a lettuce leaf, and the leaf rolled up like a filled pancake. A good combination, since the rich pork filling contrasts with the crisp lettuce.

The original version of this dish is made with squab, water chestnuts and wine, and is considered a delicacy. This recipe calls for cheaper ingredients.

With the pork, Shrimp with Cucumbers (see page 00) would make a nice contrast.

BRAISED PORK (4)

Cut into chunks

2 lbs. pork

Place it in a pot with

½ cup soy sauce
1½ cups water
¼ cup sherry
1 tablespoon brown sugar
4 stalks scallions
2 crushed cloves garlic (optional)

Cover and simmer for 1½ to 2 hours, or until done.

A very simple but good method for stewing meat.

PIG'S KNUCKLES (4)

Clean thoroughly

2 upper joints
4 pig's knuckles

Peel and crush

3 cloves garlic

or clean

3 stalks scallions

Sauté the scallions or garlic in

1 teaspoon fat

Brown the joints and knuckles over moderate heat. Then add

½ cup soy sauce
3 tablespoons brown sugar

Turn the joints and knuckles to coat them with this mixture.

When the sauce is bubbling and the joints and knuckles are absorbing the liquid, add

1 cup water

Cover and simmer over low heat for at least 1½ hours, or until the knuckles are tender and almost fall apart. Before serving, skim off the excess fat. You may also parboil

1½ lbs. spinach

by plunging the vegetables into boiling water for 3 minutes. Drain and add to the pig's knuckles. This will cut the fat in the knuckles. Serve while the spinach is still a dark green; do not let it become discolored.

A hearty, savory dish which many like because of the interesting texture of the knuckles. It is a good idea to place the knuckles on a bed of green spinach. Besides improving the taste and appearance, it makes a one-dish meal for four. Serve with rice.

MINCED PORK WITH STRING BEANS (2)

Dice

2 cups string beans

Parboil them for 5 minutes and drain. Set aside.

Chop by hand or grind

½ lb. lean pork

Beat together

2 eggs
2 tablespoons water

Set aside the eggs. Heat in a skillet over moderate flame

1½ tablespoons oil

Sauté the pork, adding

½ teaspoon salt
pepper
garlic powder (optional)

Cook for about 7 minutes, or until the pork is done. Add the string beans and mix. Add

½ cup water

Cover and cook for 2 minutes, to permit the flavors to mix. Pour in the beaten egg and stir immediately. The egg should form strands and sheets. Add

1 tablespoon corn starch mixed with ¼ cup cold water

Stir until the mixture no longer has a starchy taste.

This dish is palatable and light. It is inexpensive and may be further simplified by using a package of frozen string beans in place of fresh beans. In that case do not parboil, simply thaw the frozen beans completely before adding them to the meat.

FRESH HAM STEWED WITH CHESTNUTS (8)

Take

1 lb. chestnuts

Cut a gash in each chestnut, drop into boiling water and cook for 5 minutes. Drain and peel while hot.

Trim the fat off

1 small fresh ham

Stew the ham over low heat in the following mixture

¼ cup soy sauce
2 cups water
2 tablespoons sherry

3 tablespoons brown sugar
2 cloves garlic, crushed, or 1 teaspoon fresh ginger
2 stalks scallions

Cover and simmer for at least 2½ hours, turning the ham every half hour. Add the chestnuts during the last hour of cooking.

The chestnuts will melt in the mouth, and the ham will be rich and tasty with a molasses-like flavor. With it, for a party of eight to ten, serve:

Boned Chicken (*See page 93*)
Crabmeat Scrambled with Eggs (*See page 37*)
Beef with Mushrooms (*See page 76*)
Sautéed String Beans (*See page 120*)
Rice

FRIED PORK WITH WALNUTS (2)

Trim the fat off

¾ lb. boneless pork

Slice meat very thin and cut into ½ inch by 1½ inch pieces. Mix the meat with

1 tablespoon soy sauce
½ tablespoon brown sugar
1½ tablespoons flour

Heat in a small deep skillet

1 cup oil

When the fat is near the boiling point, add the pork, about ½ cup at a time. Do not crowd the skillet. When the pork has developed a brown crusty surface (about 5 minutes), drain on absorbent paper.

In a larger skillet place

about 1 teaspoon oil (enough to coat the pan)

Sauté

½ cup shelled walnut halves

for about 2 minutes to give them a toasted flavor. Add the fried pork, stir in

½ tablespoon soy sauce

Heat over a moderate flame for 2 or 3 minutes, or until the pork is well done.

This is a highly flavored dish and would be good with Creamed Chinese Cabbage (see page 129) and rice.

PORK BALLS (FRIED) (4)

Chop by hand, or put through a grinder

1½ lbs. pork
1 small onion
½ cup celery, or mushrooms
½ teaspoon salt
pepper

Shape the meat into balls 1 inch in diameter. Fry in moderately hot deep fat until they are brown on the outside and thoroughly cooked. Pork should never be served pink. Cut one or two open to make sure. Serve the balls plain or use them in one of the following recipes.

Rather convenient for a buffet, as they can be made ahead of time and heated when needed, as indicated in the next two recipes.

These balls are much lighter when the meat is chopped by hand, because chopping separates the fibers, whereas the grinder mashes them together. When shaping the balls, do not pack the meat too tightly. Nothing is more unpalatable than meat balls which are tough and hard.

PORK BALLS ON SPINACH (4)

Prepare by following the recipe on the preceding page

  Pork Balls

Wash and drain

  1½ lbs. spinach

Break the spinach into small pieces. To get rid of the acrid taste plunge the vegetable into

  1 quart boiling water

Drain after 2 minutes. Run cold water over the vegetable immediately and rinse it until it is completely cold. Drain. This part may be done in advance.

Sauté the spinach over high heat in

  1½ tablespoons oil
  2 cloves garlic, crushed

Add

  salt to taste
  ½ teaspoon sugar

The sugar will combat the acrid taste. Cover and cook until the spinach is dark green and tender. Add and cook until smooth

  1 tablespoon flour mixed with ½ cup water

When the floury taste is gone, add the meat balls and heat them through.

PORK BALLS WITH CHINESE CABBAGE (4)

Prepare following the recipe

Pork Balls (page 68)

Cut into 2-inch pieces

1 medium-sized stalk Chinese cabbage

Sauté the cabbage in

2 tablespoons oil

adding

½ teaspoon salt

Cover and cook for about 10 minutes over moderate heat. Thicken the juice of the cabbage with

1 tablespoon flour mixed with ¼ cup water

Cook until the starch taste disappears. Combine the pork balls with the cabbage and heat the dish through.

For a family dinner of five or six, I often make:

Chicken Soup (See page 14)
Pork Balls with Chinese Cabbage
Sautéed Squid (See page 34)
Hamburger with Peas (See page 84)
Rice (See page 138)

SWEET AND SOUR PORK (4)

Prepare following the recipe

Pork Balls (page 68)

Peel and slice as thin as possible

2 carrots

Cut into slivers

2 green peppers
1 tomato (optional)

Drain, setting aside the juice,

1 small can pineapple chunks

Heat the juice of the pineapple with

1½ tablespoons oil
3 teaspoons brown sugar
½ teaspoon salt
¼ teaspoon pepper
2 tablespoons vinegar

When the sauce is smooth and bubbling, add the carrots, pepper and tomato. Cover and cook for a few minutes. Add the pork balls and pineapple. When these ingredients are heated, thicken the sauce with

1 tablespoon flour dissolved in ¼ cup water

Stir gently and heat until the starchy taste disappears.

Somewhat lacking in subtlety, this dish nevertheless can be served during the course of a long dinner to stimulate the appetite.

PORK BALLS IN CONSOMMÉ (4)

Grind, or chop

¾ lb. pork
¼ teaspoon salt
pepper

Mix the meat with

1 egg white

Shape the meat into balls ¾ inch in diameter. Drop them into boiling

1 quart consommé

Cook for at least 10 minutes. Just before serving, add to the soup

1 teaspoon chopped scallions

Canned consommés, or homemade soups which taste flat, are greatly improved by the addition of pork.

ROAST PORK (6)

Trim the fat off

2 lbs. pork, boned

Cut the meat into strips several inches long and about 1 inch by 2 inches in cross section. Marinate the pork in the soy sauce mixture given under Barbecued Spareribs (see page 74). You may add to the mixture

maraschino cherry juice

This will give the meat its characteristic pink color. After marinating the meat for a few hours, broil the pork for 25 minutes basting every 10 minutes and placing meat 1½ inches away from high flame. Serve the pork cut into thin slices, hot or cold.

Pork by itself is never very interesting, for although it is perhaps more flavorful than beef or chicken, its texture is often too fibrous and monotonous. We usually cook it with something else, shrimp or vegetables, and in that way we get the benefit of its flavor, and vary the texture with something crisp or smooth, something light and bland. The advantage of this recipe is that you may make it in advance for a party and serve it as a cold cut, garnished with Marinated Radishes (see page 130) or some bright colored vegetables. You could also use it for canapés, as it is quite delicious in small amounts.

DICED PORK AND PEANUTS IN PUNGENT SAUCE (3)

Dice

- 2 green peppers
- 2 carrots
- ¾ lb. pork

Have ready

- ½ cup peanuts

Brown the pork in

- 2 tablespoons oil

Season the pork with

- 1½ tablespoons soy sauce

Allow some of the sauce to be absorbed by the pork, then add the diced carrots. Cover and cook for 1 or 2 minutes. Add the peanuts and peppers. Mix the ingredients and cook 3 or 4 minutes over moderate heat.

Add

- 1½ tablespoons brown sugar

Mix well and serve piping hot.

A savory dish which is simple to make, and probably new to American tables.

For a dinner for four, try:

White Cut Chicken (See page 88)
Diced Pork and Peanuts with Pungent Sauce
Sautéed Mustard Greens (See page 120)
Rice (See page 138)

BARBECUED SPARERIBS (4)

Clean

5 lbs. spareribs

and separate the ribs. Place the ribs in a large bowl and pour the following mixture over them:

2 cups soy sauce
1 cup pineapple juice
½ cup sherry
1½ tablespoons brown sugar
1 clove crushed garlic, or ½ teaspoon ground ginger

If the ribs are not completely covered by the liquid turn them occasionally. Marinate for at least half a day. Place the ribs on a broiler rack 1 inch away from medium flame and broil each side for about 7 minutes, basting with ½ cup of the soy sauce mixture. Save the rest of the marinade for future use; it will keep for a few weeks in the icebox.

You might make Plain Fried Rice (see page 140), or Rice Scrambled with Eggs (see page 139) and some Marinated Radishes (see page 130) to go with this dish.

STUFFED EGGPLANT OR YELLOW SQUASH (2)

Grind or chop

½ lb. pork
½ teaspoon salt
pepper

Wash but do not peel

1 medium-sized eggplant, or 2 yellow squash

Cut a piece off either end of the vegetable. Cut out a core about 1 inch in diameter, and fill the cavity with the meat. Replace the ends and fasten with toothpicks. Place the eggplant or squash in a pot with

1½ cups water

Cover and simmer for about ¾ hour, or until the vegetable is soft. Turn once or twice to insure even cooking. Remove the vegetable, cut it crosswise into slices about ½-inch thick. Season the liquid in the pot with

1 teaspoon monosodium glutamate
salt
pepper

Add to it

1 beaten egg yolk

Cook until the egg yolk thickens and pour over the stuffed vegetable.

The merit of this dish comes from a successful blending of flavors.

STEAMED PORK (3)

Grind or chop by hand

¾ lb. pork
½ teaspoon salt
pepper

Beat

3 eggs

Combine the meat and eggs. Place in a dish and garnish with

parsley

Place the dish in a pan of hot water and cover. Steam for at least 30 minutes, or until the pork is done.

Chopped or ground meat often tends to become tough and heavy. The addition of eggs makes this dish light.

With this dish I would serve Fish with Pungent Sauce (see page 42) and Zucchini (see page 24), Rice (see page 138).

PORK OR BEEF WITH MUSHROOMS (3)

Wash and cut into slices

½ lb. mushrooms

Cut into thin slivers

1 lb. pork, or beef

Chop

2 stalks scallions

Sauté the scallions in

2 tablespoons oil

When they begin to brown add the meat. Stir and add

1 tablespoon soy sauce

When the meat is half done (3 minutes for pork, 2 minutes for beef), remove from pan and set aside. Sauté the mushrooms in the juice of the meat, adding a little more oil if necessary. When the mushrooms become moist and tender, add the meat. Combine, cover and cook over moderate heat until done (about 2 more minutes).

Here is a recipe for mushroom fanciers. Many people miss the mild flavor of mushrooms because it is often lost among many other ingredients. We like mushrooms because of their uniqueness: being neither meat nor vegetable, their taste is different, their texture unusual. Do not overcook the mushrooms or they will wither and lose their juices.

BROCCOLI WITH BEEF (2)

Prepare as directed below

    1½ cups broccoli

Wash and drain them in a sieve or colander. Slice thin

    ½ lb. steak

To keep the beef moist and tender, dredge the slices with

    1 tablespoon corn starch, or flour

Then moisten them with

    1 tablespoon soy sauce

Heat in a skillet over highest flame

    3 tablespoons oil

Sauté the beef in the hot skillet for 2 minutes. Remove the beef before it is quite done. Leave the juices behind and add the broccoli. Sprinkle the vegetable with

    ½ teaspoon salt
    ⅓ cup water

Cover the skillet for about 4 minutes, stirring occasionally. Finish cooking the broccoli *uncovered,* else it will turn yellow; this will take 1 or 2 more minutes, depending on the tenderness of the broccoli.

Now add the beef and season with

1 teaspoon monosodium glutamate

When the beef is done, serve at once.

Broccoli stems are edible if peeled. The hard green fibers may be removed with a small sharp knife, leaving the light green tender cores. Slice the stems on the diagonal into pieces ¼-inch thick. Cut the flowerets into two. You may discard the stems if they are too tough, and use only the flowerets.

STEAK CUBES (4)

Remove the steak from the refrigerator at least an hour before cooking.

Trim off the fat from

1½ lbs. steak

Remove the bone and cut the steak into large cubes, about 1½ inches on each side. Moisten the steak cubes with

1 tablespoon soy sauce
½ teaspoon monosodium glutamate
pepper

Wash and cut into small pieces

½ lb. mushrooms
½ stalk celery
2 small yellow onions

Brown the onions over high heat in

1½ tablespoons oil

Add the steak and stir immediately. The meat should brown very quickly. Remove the meat after a minute or two; it should be only half done at this point.

Sauté the mushrooms over moderate heat, adding

1 tablespoon oil

if they become dry. Add the celery and sauté for a few minutes, adding a little

salt

Turn the heat to high, add the steak and mix. Remove from heat when the steak is as well done or rare as you like it.

Use the very best steak for this.

ANISEED BEEF (5)

Cut into 1½-inch cubes (or leave whole if this is to be served cold)

2 lbs. shank beef

Cook the beef over a slow fire for about 10 minutes in the following mixture:

½ cup soy sauce
1½ tablespoons brown sugar
1½ tablespoons sherry
4 cloves aniseed, tied in cheesecloth

Gradually add

1 cup water

Cover and simmer for 2 hours, turning occasionally. If the water evaporates add a little more. The liquid should come up to half the level of the meat. Remove the aniseed when the meat is tender.

If this is to be served cold, follow the recipe, then cool the beef and place it in the refrigerator; the liquid will jell. Slice the meat as thin as possible, use it for cold cuts, sandwiches, or as an appetizer.

BEEF STEWED WITH SOY SAUCE (5)

Prepare following the recipe on the preceding page

Aniseed Beef

Omit the aniseed.

This is a plain way of cooking beef, suitable for family dinners with:

Fresh Scallops (See page 32)
Beef Stewed with Soy Sauce
Sautéed Tomatoes, Cucumbers (See page 121)
Rice (See page 138)

BEEF CURRY (4)

Cut into chunks

1½ lbs. stewing beef
4 white onions
4 medium-sized potatoes (optional)

Sauté the onions for a few minutes with

1½ tablespoons oil
1 teaspoon curry (or more, according to taste)
1 teaspoon salt

When the onions are lightly browned, add the beef. Mix well and cook for about 3 minutes. Add

1½ cups water

Cover and simmer for about 1½ hours, or until the beef is tender, adding the potatoes for the last 40 minutes of cooking. If potatoes are omitted, serve with

Boiled Rice (see page 138)

BEEF WITH ASPARAGUS TIPS (2)

Cut into slivers

¾ lb. steak

Dredge the beef with

2 tablespoons flour

Moisten the slivers with

2 tablespoons soy sauce

Cut with a diagonal motion into 1-inch sections, using only the green parts

1½ lbs. asparagus

Sauté the beef in a very hot skillet with

2 tablespoons oil

When the meat is half done (about 2 minutes), remove the slivers and set aside. Sauté the asparagus in

1 tablespoon oil

Add

½ teaspoon salt
1 to 2 tablespoons water

Cover and cook until crisp (5 minutes). When the asparagus turns bright green, add the beef and combine (2 more minutes). Serve immediately.

The merit of this dish lies in the skill of the cook. Half of the technique of Chinese cooking is knowing when to add what, and when to stop cooking the ingredients. Read the short introduction to this section before making this dish.

Timing is very important; remember to remove the beef from the skillet when it is not completely done. Quickly sauté the asparagus in the juices left behind, and finish cooking the beef when you combine it with the asparagus.

BEEF WITH CELERY (2)

Follow the recipe on the preceding page for

    Beef with Asparagus Tips

Substitute for the asparagus

    1 small stalk celery

Dice the celery.

One of my stand-bys. This dish can be varied by substituting pork for the beef. All you need is this and rice (see page 00) to make a meal for two.

BEEF STEW (4)

Cut into 1½-inch cubes

    1½ lbs. shank beef

Crush

    2 cloves garlic

and brown them in

    4 tablespoons oil

Then mix in

    4 tablespoons soy sauce

Now add the cubed beef and sauté briefly over high heat, to brown the meat.

Reduce the heat, and add

3 tablespoons water

Cover and simmer for 1 hour, adding a little more water if necessary. Simmer over low heat. Meanwhile peel and cut into chunks

4 carrots
4 medium-sized potatoes

Add the carrots and potatoes to the meat, which should be fairly tender at this point. Add

1 cup water

Cover and simmer for ½ hour more.

Soy sauce adds a great deal of flavor to an indifferent cut of meat. I usually make this for the family, along with rice and another vegetable, for a simple wholesome meal.

BEEF WITH TOMATOES, CELERY, AND PEPPERS (4)

Trim and slice very thin

1½ lbs. steak

If the meat appears tough, dredge it with

3 tablespoons flour, or corn starch
pepper

Moisten it with

1½ tablespoons soy sauce

If the steak is tender omit this step; add the soy sauce when the beef is being sautéed.

Cut into small pieces and set aside

2 cups celery, tomatoes, green peppers and onions in any proportion

Sauté the beef over highest heat in

2 tablespoons oil

When the beef is half done (about 3 minutes), remove it from the skillet and set aside. Leave the liquid in the pan and add the onions, celery, peppers and tomatoes in the order given. Add to the vegetables

½ teaspoon salt
½ teaspoon monosodium glutamate

Sauté over high heat, mixing gently but thoroughly. Cook until the peppers are bright green; the celery and peppers should be crisp. Add the beef, mix gently until done (1-2 minutes).

Vary the ingredients according to the materials on hand. This is an everyday dish which can be excellent if your technique in sautéing is right.

Popular with friends and family. To serve five you could cook

Beef with Tomatoes, Celery, and Peppers
Braised Chicken (*See page 95*)
Lettuce and Green Peppers, sautéed (*See page 120*)
Rice (*See page 138*)

HAMBURGER WITH PEAS (3)

Chop

1 yellow onion

Brown the onion in

1½ tablespoons oil

Add to the onion

1½ lbs. ground round steak, broken up

Maintain moderately high heat and sauté the meat until it is half done (2-3 minutes). Add

1 tablespoon soy sauce

When the liquid is partly absorbed add

1 package frozen peas (completely thawed)

Mix, cook uncovered for about 4 minutes.

If you want to prepare a simple and quick meal, you can add 2 cups cold cooked *rice (see page 139) to the hamburger and peas. Quickly made, attractive and nourishing.*

STRING BEANS AND BEEF (2)

If fresh string beans are used, wash, break off the tips and sliver

1½ cups string beans

or use

1 box frozen string beans

Trim off all the fat and bone from

¾ lb. steak

Slice the steak very thin. Chop or slice

1 medium-sized yellow onion

Brown the onion in

2 tablespoons butter or oil

When the skillet is very hot, add the beef. Sauté quickly over highest heat for 2 minutes. Add

2 tablespoons soy sauce

Stir. Immediately remove the meat, leaving juices behind. Add the beans to the juice and sauté for 5 to 6 minutes for fresh string beans, 3 minutes for the frozen kind. Now add the beef, mix gently to combine for about 1 more minute, or until the beef is done. Stop cooking at once and serve.

The thinner the beef is cut, the more flavorful and tender it will be. Use French style frozen string beans if you wish to save time. Thaw them out completely and drain on absorbent paper.

SAUTÉED KIDNEYS (2)

Rub with a lot of salt

4 pork kidneys

and remove the membranes. Wash off the salt by repeated rinsing and wipe dry with a cloth or towel. Slice the kidney, avoiding the central part. Place all the slices on a board close together, and slash them lightly and quickly with a long sharp knife, making diamond patterns. In this manner a greater surface area is obtained and the heat will penetrate more quickly. Wash and cut into pieces

1 stalk leeks, or 3 stalks scallions

Sauté them in a hot skillet with

2 tablespoons oil

Permit the skillet to become extremely hot. Add the kidneys and stir immediately. Sauté them for almost 1 minute, then add

1 tablespoon sherry, or brandy

When most of the alcohol has evaporated add

1 tablespoon soy sauce

Stir and mix constantly. Serve immediately when the kidneys are done. This should take no more than 4 or 5 minutes.

The kidneys have to be as dry as possible before being cooked. Kidneys are considered a delicacy in China, and moreover they are very nourishing. High heat and quick cooking give this dish a wonderful texture.

SAUTÉED LIVER (2)

Slice thin

¾ lb. calves' liver, or pork liver

Wash, split down the middle and cut into 1-inch sections

2 stalks leeks

Sauté the leeks in a very hot skillet with

2 tablespoons oil

When they are lightly browned at the edges, add the liver all at once, and maintain high heat, stirring constantly for 3 to 4 minutes. Pour in

1 tablespoon cooking sherry

Continue stirring. When the sherry has partially evaporated add

1½ tablespoons soy sauce

Serve immediately.

Liver cooked this way will not become dry and grainy. It should be rather resilient in texture, tasty and not at all bloody looking.

6

Fowl

WHITE CUT CHICKEN

Method I (4)

Clean

1 plump roasting chicken (about 3 lbs.)

Tie the legs and wings as for roasting. Heat enough water to cover the bird, about 3 quarts. Add to the water

2 slices fresh ginger, or ¼ teaspoon pepper
1 tablespoon salt

When the water is boiling vigorously, place the chicken in it, cover the pot and maintain moderately high heat. Remove the chicken after 25 or 30 minutes. When cold, chop the chicken into small pieces 1 inch by 2 inches. Serve it cold with

soy sauce
Chinese parsley
chopped scallions

The success of this dish depends on the quality of the chicken. Buy only the best, the plumpest chicken, preferably one with a thin layer of fat below the skin.

Method II (2)

Clean and truss

1 broiler (about 2 lbs.)

Heat enough water to cover the chicken, adding

1 teaspoon salt
¼ teaspoon pepper

Place the chicken in the boiling water, cover and turn the heat off. Remove the chicken in 30 minutes. Cool and serve as directed above.

This recipe calls for smaller, more tender chickens.

Note:
Frozen Chicken will not be satisfactory for White Cut Chicken, Soy Sauce Chicken (see page 92) and "Drunk" Chicken (see page 101) since these require plump fowl which have very tender white meat and a thin layer of fat below the skin. You can, however, use frozen chicken for all the sautéed dishes. Boned chicken meat may be troublesome to prepare, unless you use frozen chicken breasts, which are easy to bone when they are thawed out. You can also buy chicken breasts from poultry-in-parts stores; the white meat is more tender than dark when sautéed.

CHICKEN IN JELLY (4)

Prepare following the receipe on the preceding page

1 (1½-lb.) broiler

Bone the chicken and cut it into thin slices or pieces. Prepare the following:

2 teaspoons chopped parsley
¼ cup chopped or slivered ham
¼ cup finely chopped celery
⅛ cup sliced radishes
¼ cup diced cucumbers

Drain

1 small can canned asparagus
1 medium can canned mushrooms

Set aside the liquids. Place the chicken and other ingredients in a ring or other mold to make an attractive dish. Soften

2 packages gelatin

in

½ cup water

Heat

1 cup liquid (canned chicken soup, water, or the liquid from the asparagus and mushrooms)

Dissolve the gelatin in the hot liquid, adding

salt
pepper
monosodium glutamate

When all the gelatin has dissolved add

2½ cups canned chicken soup, or water

Pour the gelatin mixture over the ingredients in the mold. Chill. When the jelly is firm run a knife along the side of the mold and invert it. Serve the jelly garnished with lettuce and radishes.

Variation I

A very pretty effect may be obtained by making the jelly with a little soy sauce. Use radishes, parsley and the white meat of the chicken to contrast with the brown jelly. Prepare the ingredients as directed. Omit the salt, pepper and monosodium glutamate from the gelatin mixture and substitute

¼ cup soy sauce

for ¼ cup of the liquid.

For a buffet for eight the following menu is attractive and fairly easy:

Chicken in Jelly
Shrimp on Toast (See page 52)
Curried Beef (See page 80)
Fried Pork with Walnuts (See page 67)

Mixed Vegetables *(See page 127)*
Rice *(See page 138)*

SOY SAUCE CHICKEN (4)

Clean

1 roasting chicken (about 3 lbs.)

Wipe it dry and truss as for roasting.
Heat over a moderate flame to the boiling point

1 cup soy sauce
1 cup water
½ cup brown sugar
1 cup cooking sherry
4 stalks scallions, chopped

Place the chicken in the boiling liquid, cover and cook over moderate heat for 35 to 40 minutes, turning the chicken once or twice to brown it evenly. Remove and cool the chicken. Just before serving chop it into small pieces, or bone and slice it. Serve the soy sauce mixture with it.

A variation on White Cut Chicken. The sauce may be saved and used over again. Store it in the refrigerator.

When using the soy sauce mixture again, add a little more sherry, sugar and soy sauce in the proportions given above. This is a good dish to serve as the main course in an American dinner, with Spinach and Mushrooms (see page 127) Rice (see page 138), preceded by a Beef Soup (see page 20).

BONELESS CHICKEN WITH VEGETABLES (4)

Prepare following the recipe for White Cut Chicken (see page 88)

1 (3-lb.) roasting chicken

When the chicken is cold, bone it and cut it neatly into small pieces 1 inch by 2 inches, or slice it into thin pieces. Cut

½ lb. Canadian bacon, or ham

into pieces of the same size as the chicken. Place the bacon and the chicken alternately on a platter. When ready to serve pour the sauce* over the meat. Surround the meat with

asparagus, mustard greens, or broccoli

To Prepare Vegetables

Wash

2 lbs. asparagus, 1½ lbs. broccoli, or 1 lb. mustard greens

Use only the tender parts of the vegetable. Cut the vegetable into pieces 1½ inches long. Boil

2½ quarts water

Drop the vegetables into the boiling water, but do not cover. Cook the vegetable until it is vivid green and partly tender. Broccoli should take about 10 minutes, asparagus about 12 minutes, and the mustard greens about 8 minutes. Drain immediately into a colander and run cold water over the vegetable until it is completely cold. Drain thoroughly.

** Sauce*

Heat

2 teaspoons oil

Add and mix until smooth

2 teaspoons flour, or corn starch

Stir in slowly

¾ cup water
1 teaspoon monosodium glutamate
½ teaspoon salt

When the mixture is smooth and bubbling, add in a thin stream

2 egg yolks beaten with ¼ cup water

Maintain low heat and stir until smooth and creamy.

A very attractive dish. The meat and vegetables may all be prepared well in advance. The sauce is poured over the dish just before serving.

Menu for a party of six:

Boned Chicken
Sautéed Pike (See page 44)
Minced Pork (See page 63)
Sautéed Chinese Cabbage (See page 120)
Rice (See page 138)

CHICKEN STEWED WITH CHESTNUTS (4)

Clean and chop into 2-inch sections

1 roasting chicken (about 2½ lbs.)

Prepare according to the rule under Fresh Ham Stewed with Chestnuts (see page 66)

½ lb. chestnuts

Brown the chicken pieces in

3 tablespoons oil

seasoning with

1½ tablespoons soy sauce, or ¾ teaspoon salt

After the chicken has been sautéed for a few minutes, add

2 tablespoons sherry

Evaporate some of the alcohol, then add the chestnuts and add

3 tablespoons water

Cover closely and stew over low heat until the chestnuts are tender (about 45 minutes.)

This doesn't appear very often in family dinners, because of the work involved in preparing the chestnuts. It is for holiday feasts or elaborate dinners.

BRAISED CHICKEN (4)

Wash and dry

½ lb. mushroom caps

Clean and wipe dry

2 small broilers, or 1 large roasting chicken

Chop up the chicken into small pieces, about 1½ inches in length. Peel, and chop or crush

3 cloves garlic

Brown the garlic in a moderately hot skillet in

3 tablespoons oil

When the flavor is extracted from the garlic, remove the browned pieces. Turn the heat to high, add the chicken and brown the pieces lightly; this will take about 10 minutes. Add the mushrooms, reduce the heat slightly, cover and cook for about 5 minutes. Add

1½ tablespoons sherry

When the sherry has been partly absorbed add

2 tablespoons soy sauce, or ½ teaspoon salt and 1 tablespoon water

1½ teaspoons monosodium glutamate

Cover the skillet and cook for about 10 minutes, or until the chicken is tender.

When this is being prepared a wonderful "perfume," a blend of garlic, sherry and chicken, seems to fill the air. This is one of my stand-bys.

BRAISED CHICKEN WINGS (6)

Clean and wipe dry

1½ lbs. chicken wings

Prepare the soy sauce mixture as for Soy Sauce Chicken (see page 92). Place the wings in the cold liquid, heat to boiling and simmer for about ¾ hour or until the wings are very tender. Remove from sauce and serve hot or cold.

This is eaten for fun. It will not satisfy hunger.

The Chinese regard chicken wings as a delicacy because of the fine texture of the meat and the slippery quality of the skin.

VELVET CHICKEN (5 or 6)

Wash and cut into small pieces to permit quick cooking

¼ cup walnuts, or almonds
½ cup sliced mushrooms
¾ cup peas-in-the-pod (snow peas)
½ cup string beans, sliced or diced
½ cup celery

Drain and set aside.

Bone and skin

1 (4-lb.) roasting chicken (or 4 frozen chicken breasts)

Cut the meat into thin slices, place on a board and pound lightly with the dull edge of a chopping knife.

Beat until frothy

2 egg whites
½ teaspoon salt
½ teaspoon monosodium glutamate
pepper

Mix the egg white with the chicken slices. Heat in a skillet

2 tablespoons vegetable oil
2 slices fresh ginger, or ¼ teaspoon ground ginger

When the skillet is extremely hot add the chicken and stir at once. The meat should turn white in less than 1 minute. If it does not do so, the skillet is not hot enough. Remove the meat after 2 or 3 minutes, leaving the juices in the pan. Maintain high heat and sauté the other ingredients, adding

½ teaspoon salt
1 tablespoon oil (if necessary)

When the vegetables are bright green add the chicken and mix gently. Do not overcook.

White meat is more tender than dark meat when prepared in the above manner; for economy's sake, however, you may use all of the chicken.

CHICKEN IN WAX PAPER (4)

Bone

1 roasting chicken, or broiler (about 3 lbs.)

Slice the meat into pieces 1½ inches by 2 inches. Sprinkle the pieces with a little

garlic salt, or celery salt
pepper
monosodium glutamate

or moisten the chicken with

1½ tablespoons soy sauce

Cut pieces of wax paper 4 inches square. Wrap each slice of chicken in a piece of paper, tucking the ends in firmly. Fry the packages in deep fat for 5 minutes, or until done. Serve the meat in the paper just as it comes out of the fryer.

A gourmet's dish. Aluminum foil may be used instead of wax paper.

The juices of the chicken are sealed in by the wax paper.

CARAWAY CHICKEN (2)

Clean and singe any hairs off

1 (1½-lb.) fryer

Cut the chicken into sections. Dry them with a paper towel. Coat them with

2 tablespoons soy sauce

Mix the following and place in a paper bag

¾ cup flour
1 teaspoon caraway seed

Dredge the chicken with flour by placing the pieces in the bag, a few at a time, and shaking the bag. Fry the chicken in hot deep fat until brown, about 15 minutes. Drain on paper. Sprinkle the pieces with

½ teaspoon caraway seed

Delicious and unusual. Please try this recipe.

For two:

Cucumber Soup *(See page 23)*
Caraway Chicken
Eggplant, Tomatoes, and Bacon *(See page 129)*

For four:

Caraway Chicken
Sliced Lamb with Leeks *(See page 62)*
Sautéed String Beans *(See page 120)*
Rice *(See page 138)*

CHICKEN CURRY WITH CREAM (6)

Cut into sections

2 (1½-lb.) fryers, or broilers

Heat in a deep skillet

3 tablespoons oil, or butter
1 tablespoon curry (or more according to taste)

Sauté the chicken in the fat, adding

1 teaspoon salt

When the pieces are lightly coated with the curry, add

½ cup water

Cover closely and simmer for about 25 minutes. Maintain low heat and slowly stir in

2 cups cream or rich milk, in which 2 tablespoons corn starch have been dissolved

Serve immediately when the cream has been sufficiently heated. *Do not* allow cream to boil.

This is often served with side dishes of coconut, chopped peanuts, chutney, chopped hard-boiled eggs, raisins and parsley. The curry is spooned over hot Chinese style rice (see page 138) and the plate liberally sprinkled with the "trimmings."

For a Dish to serve with this see last page.

CHICKEN CURRY (3)

Clean and chop into 1½-inch pieces remove skin &

1 (2-lb.) broiler, or fryer bones

Cut into chunks

med. 2 ~~or 3~~ white onions large chunks

~~4 potatoes (optional)~~*

Sauté the onions in

3 tablespoons oil

2 ~~1~~ tablespoon curry (or more according to taste)

Add the chicken and mix thoroughly. Cover for a few minutes, then add 1½ cups water.

Simmer over low heat for about 10 minutes. Add

1 teaspoon salt - 1/4 tsp. pepper

~~the potatoes~~

Cook for 20 minutes more, ~~or until the potatoes are tender.~~

Excellant dish with above corrections.

* *This dish is best served with rice (see page 138).*

FRIED CHICKEN LIVERS AND GIBLETS (4)

Clean and wipe dry with a towel

1 cup chicken livers

1 cup chicken giblets

Cut up each giblet into 3 pieces, and with a sharp knife make several gashes in each piece. This permits faster cooking. Dredge the pieces with

flour

Heat to the boiling point

3 cups oil

Fry about ½ cup at a time, until the pieces are brown. Drain on absorbent paper and serve immediately, sprinkling liberally with

salt-and-pepper mix
lemon juice (optional)

These are lovely with cocktails. In a Chinese dinner they usually come as part of the hors d'oeuvres.

"DRUNK" CHICKEN (4)

Clean and truss

1 (2-lb.) tender spring chicken

Heat to boiling

3 quarts water
1 teaspoon salt

When the water is rapidly boiling, place the chicken in it; cover and turn the heat off. Permit the water and the chicken to cool to room temperature, away from the stove. When the water is cold, remove the chicken and drain. Place it in a large bowl or in a large glass jar. Cover the chicken completely with

sherry

Cover the bowl or jar closely and keep in the refrigerator for about 1 week. When ready to serve, chop up the chicken into small pieces. This is to be served cold. Keep the sherry in the refrigerator for future use.

Called "drunk" because the chicken is immersed in a wine bath for a week, during which time it becomes impregnated with the wine and acquires an incomparable flavor. This is a good dish to serve with wine. Eat it slowly to enjoy its taste.

For a party of six to eight:

Crabmeat Soufflé *(See page 38)*
"Drunk" Chicken
Mushrooms Stuffed with Pork and Shrimp *(See page 50)*
Beef with Asparagus Tips *(See page 81)*
Rice *(See page 138)*

CHICKEN WITH PEPPERS (2)

Remove seeds, rinse and dice enough peppers to make

½ cup green peppers
½ cup red peppers

Clean, dry and bone

1 (1½-lb.) fryer or broiler

Cut up the meat into ½-inch cubes. To give a velvety texture, dip the chicken in:

2 egg whites beaten with 1½ tablespoons corn starch

Heat thoroughly

2 tablespoons oil

When the skillet is extremely hot, add the chicken all at once. Stir immediately. Sauté for 2 or 3 minutes, then add

1 tablespoon sherry

When the skillet is again very hot add

2 tablespoons soy sauce, or 1 teaspoon salt
1 teaspoon sugar
½ teaspoon Tabasco

Stir constantly for about 5 minutes, or until the chicken is almost done and the juices are bubbling. Add the diced peppers and cook for about 4 more minutes.

A very fine dish if properly cooked. The peppers must be crisp, the chicken tender and the sauce rich and hot. Both red and green peppers are used for their color.

CHICKEN WITH ZUCCHINI OR CUCUMBERS (2)

Bone and dice

1 (2-lb.) chicken, or 2 chicken breasts (fresh or frozen)

Peel, wash and dice

1½ cups zucchini, or cucumbers

Crush

2 cloves garlic

and sauté them in

3½ tablespoons oil

When the skillet is very hot, and not before, add the chicken. Sauté for 3 to 4 minutes over high heat. Then add

2 tablespoons soy sauce, or ¾ teaspoon salt
½ teaspoon monosodium glutamate

Add the vegetable, cover and cook for a few more minutes. Thicken the juices with

1 tablespoon corn starch dissolved in ¼ cup water

Cook until the floury taste is gone (about 1 minute).

A light dish for summer. Melons, as well as leafy vegetables, may be cooked with chicken. If you are using cucumbers, be sure to stop cooking them while they are still somewhat crisp.

CHICKEN WITH CAULIFLOWER (2)

Wash and cut into flowerets

    1 small head cauliflower

Parboil them for 3 minutes. Drain.
Chop into 1½-inch pieces

    1 (1½-lb.) fryer

Heat in a skillet

    2 tablespoons oil
    2 stalks scallions, chopped

When the edges of the scallions are brown, add the chicken and sauté over high heat for about 8 minutes, adding

    ½ teaspoon salt, or 2 tablespoons soy sauce
    ½ teaspoon monosodium glutamate

Cover, reduce heat and cook for another 6 minutes. Add the cauliflower and cook for about 6 minutes more, covered. Add water if necessary.
When the cauliflower is barely soft and the chicken is done, thicken the gravy with

    1 tablespoon corn starch dissolved in ¼ cup water

Heat for 2 more minutes.

This can be quite excellent. It is made with common ingredients. Stop when cauliflower is just tender enough to bite into. Don't cook it until it is completely soft.

CHICKEN WITH ALMONDS (3)

Bone and slice into slivers

1 (2-lb.) broiler (fresh or frozen)

Chop coarsely

½ cup blanched and toasted almonds

Have ready

4 unbeaten egg whites

Heat in a skillet

2½ tablespoons oil

When the skillet is extremely hot, add the chicken. Sauté it quickly adding

pepper
¾ teaspoon salt
1 tablespoon cooking sherry

Maintain high heat for 3-4 minutes. Add the egg white, and scramble the mixture. When the egg white is set, add the almonds and heat the dish through. Serve immediately. Sprinkle with some more

salt

You can use cocktail peanuts in place of the almonds. In that case, use less salt.

A light, delicious dish. The skillet must be as hot as possible when the egg white is added.

DUCK WITH CHINESE CABBAGE (4)

Clean and wipe dry

1 (4-5 lb.) duck

removing the oil sacks. Discard the neck. Truss the bird and place it on a roasting rack over a large pan. Roast the duck in a hot oven (400° F.) for at least ½ hour, or until the duck is lightly browned and a large portion of the fat has been extracted. Remove the duck from the oven and season it with

1½ teaspoons salt
½ teaspoon ground ginger

Simmer the duck covered for 2 hours in

2½ cups water

Adding more water as needed.

Cut into 2-inch pieces

1 large head Chinese cabbage

Smother the duck with the cabbage and cover (first removing any excess fat). Simmer covered for at least 1 more hour. The flavor of this dish is improved with long simmering. The duck will probably be too soft to be served whole. We usually serve this dish in the pot in which it is cooked.

A superb combination. It is best to cook this dish with a lean bird; in any case much of the fat should be extracted from the duck before it is combined with the cabbage.

ROAST DUCK WITH PINEAPPLE

Choose a lean, plump

4 lb. duck or two small ducks

Clean, truss and roast the duck in a moderate oven until done. The skin should be golden brown. Cool. Bone it. This should be simple if the duck is well done. Separate the legs from the body and bone them, cutting the meat neatly into pieces about 1½ inches long and 1 inch wide. Discard the wings.

With a small sharp knife remove the "oysters." Bone the breast by cutting along the midline, and slipping the knife between the meat and the bone. Cut the meat into pieces about 1 inch wide. Discard the carcass.

Drain, saving the juice

1 can pineapple slices

Cut each pineapple ring into four pieces. Place the oysters and the meat from the legs in a shallow ovenproof dish. Place the breast meat on top and sprinkle the entire dish with

salt

Garnish with pineapple. Heat the following in a saucepan

the pineapple juice
2 tablespoons salad oil
2 tablespoons soy sauce
1 tablespoon brandy or sherry
½ cup water
2 tablespoons brown sugar

Pour the mixture over the duck. Cover loosely with aluminum foil or wax paper. Heat in a moderate oven 350 degrees for about 1 hour.

The duck may be roasted in advance. This is an excellent company dish as it may be kept in the oven without spoiling the flavor. Serve it with white or wild rice and a salad, if you are giving an American dinner.

MINCED SQUAB ON LETTUCE

Variation I (2)

Clean and wipe dry

3 squabs

Remove the bones and save them for soup. Chop the meat by hand until extremely fine, with

½ cup bamboo shoots
½ cup water chestnuts

Heat in a skillet

1½ tablespoons oil
½ teaspoon ginger

Maintain high heat and add the squab mixture, stirring constantly and mixing well. After a few minutes add

1 tablespoon brandy, or whiskey

Sauté until done, about 8 to 10 minutes. Add at the very last

½ teaspoon salt

Serve with

whole lettuce leaves

Variation II (3)

You may increase the bulk and vary the flavor of this dish by adding

½ cup mushrooms
½ cup celery

Chop these ingredients together with the squab.

A perfectly delicious, if expensive, combination. I like the lettuce leaves to be ice cold, but the squab should be very hot. The lettuce leaves should be fresh and large, so that the squab may be wrapped up in them. The squab may be a bit oily by itself, but this is modified by the taste of lettuce. We usually fill the leaf with about two tablespoons of squab, and roll it up like a pancake.

FRIED SQUAB (2)

Clean and wipe dry

2 squabs

Fry the squabs in deep hot fat for about 20 to 30 minutes, or until the skin turns a deep brown. Drain on absorbent paper. When cool enough to handle, chop each squab into 6 or 8 pieces. Serve on lettuce with

lemon slices
salt-and-pepper mix (page 134)

The squab is fried whole and then chopped into smaller pieces. In this way the juices are retained.

BRAISED SQUAB (2)

Clean and wipe dry

2 squabs

Cut each squab into 4 pieces. Heat in a skillet

1½ tablespoon oil

Add the squab and maintain moderate heat. Sauté briefly and cover. Turn occasionally. Season with

⅛ teaspoon ground ginger

When the squab is browned add

2 tablespoons brandy, sherry, or whiskey

Turn the heat to low. When the liquor has partially evaporated, sprinkle with

½ teaspoon salt, or 1 tablespoon soy sauce

Cover and cook for 20 to 25 minutes in all, or until tender.

Squab is supposed to be very nourishing and is often given to invalids or sick people to make them strong. Invalid or not, almost everyone will like this.

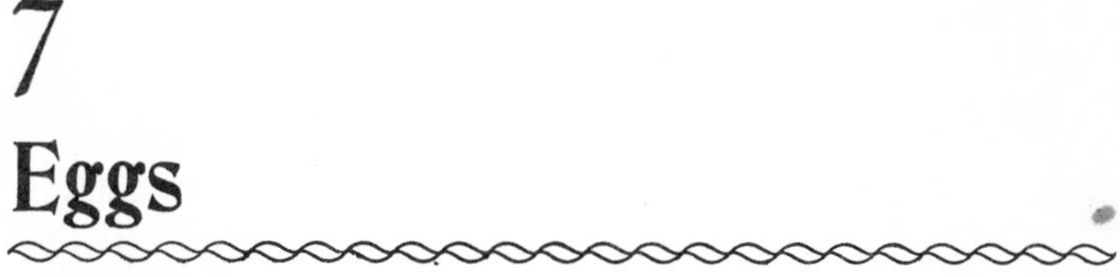

7
Eggs

SOY SAUCE EGGS

Prepare the sauce given under Soy Sauce Chicken (see page 92). Omit the sherry. There should be enough sauce to cover the eggs.

Soft boil

eggs

by placing them in boiling water for 4 minutes. Remove the eggs immediately and cool them under the water tap. The cold will make the membrane stick to the shell rather than the white of the egg. Place the shelled eggs in the boiling

soy sauce mixture

Cover and cook for 4 minutes. Drain, setting aside the liquid. When cool cut into slices or quarters. The soy sauce mixture may be stored in the refrigerator for future use.

These are fine to serve with cold cuts and salads, or in sandwiches. Do not overcook the eggs; otherwise they will shrink and the yolks will be too dry.

STEAMED EGGS (2)

Beat

4 eggs
½ cup liquid (water, or juice from canned mushrooms)
salt
pepper

Place the egg mixture in a deep dish or bowl. Set it in a pan of water. Cover and cook on top of stove for at least 30 minutes, or until the center is set.

Not unlike a custard. The addition of water to the eggs makes them light. This is a delicately flavored dish which may be varied by the addition of mushrooms, ham, parsley, celery. In any case the ingredients added should be finely chopped so that they will not sink to the bottom of the dish.

FRIED EGGS WITH SOY SAUCE

Heat in a skillet

oil (about ½ tablespoon to 1 egg)

When the skillet is very hot, break

eggs

into skillet. Brown both sides. Do not overcook; the yolk must still be liquid. Just before removing the eggs from the pan pour over each egg

½ teaspoon soy sauce

Sprinkle the yolk with

pepper

Heat ½ minute longer and serve immediately.

Chinese fry eggs over high heat; hence the eggs often have a crisp crusty surface.

TEA LEAF EGGS

Boil

3 cups water

Place in a pot

3 tablespoons red Ceylon tea

Add the boiling water, cover and let stand for 10 minutes. Soft boil

eggs

for 4 minutes. Drain. Crack the shells by gently rolling and pressing the eggs on a board. Heat the tea to boiling and place the cracked eggs in it. Cover and cook for about 15 minutes. Drain, cool and shell the eggs.

You may like the unusual flavor which the tea imparts to the eggs. Cracking the shells before placing the eggs in the tea produces a marbled effect.

EGG TURNOVERS WITH HAM (4)

Chop together

- ¼ lb. ham
- ¼ lb. mushrooms, drained (canned or fresh)
- parsley

Beat until light

- 6 eggs
- ¼ teaspoon salt

Heat gently in a skillet

- 1 tablespoon oil

Place about 2 tablespoons egg mixture in the skillet. When the egg is partly set, place 1 teaspoon of the ham mixture on top of the egg. Fold the egg in half, covering the ham mixture. Press lightly with a spatula. The meat should be sealed in. Remove from the skillet.

Keep the turnovers hot by placing them on a plate which is set over a pot of boiling water. Keep the plate covered.

These are often made for parties as they will keep without damage. They will look prettier if served on a bed of lettuce. You might also surround them with some sautéed vegetables.

EGG TURNOVERS WITH FRESH PORK (2)

Chop fine by hand, or put through the grinder

- ¼ lb. lean pork

⅛ cup celery
¼ teaspoon salt

Beat together

4 eggs
¼ teaspoon salt

Proceed as in Egg Turnovers with Ham (see page 114). Place a teaspoonful of the pork mixture on the partly set egg. Fold the egg over in half and press lightly. When all the turnovers have been made, arrange them in a skillet. Add

3 tablespoons water

Cover and cook over moderate heat for about 8 minutes, or until the pork is done and the water has been absorbed.

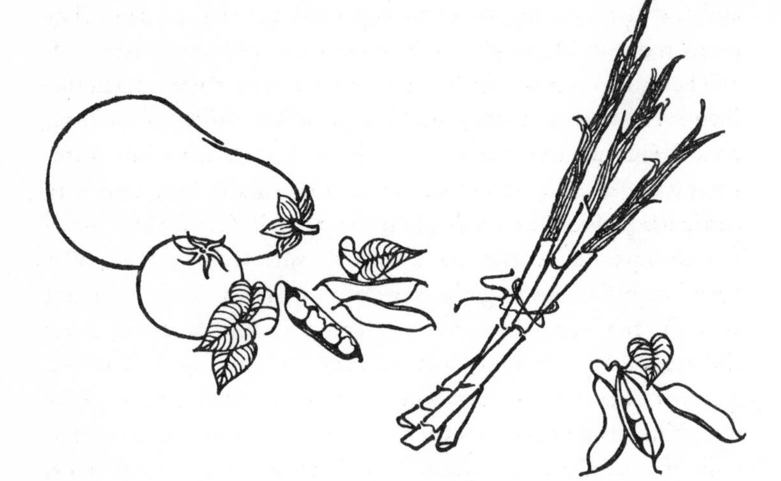

8

Vegetables

VEGETABLES should be eaten for their crispness, their color and their taste. When they are cooked, be careful to preserve all three qualities.

The first rule to follow is never to overcook them. You will be able to tell when to stop cooking a vegetable by looking at its color. When a vegetable is cooked, its color will turn successively bright green, dark green, then olive-colored. Stop cooking the vegetable when it is somewhere between the bright and dark green stages. Never let it become discolored. In this way you will find that not only the color, but the taste and the crispness of the fresh vegetable are still present. The result is not unlike a salad in its appeal and attractiveness.

The usual Chinese method of cooking vegetables is to sautée them. This means to fry quickly in a hot skillet with little grease. Cut up the washed and drained vegetables into bite-size pieces. Heat a tablespoon or so of oil in a skillet. You may add garlic, onion, or fresh ginger to the oil. Sauté them for a few minutes to extract the flavor. Be sure to have the skillet very hot before adding the vegetable. If the skillet is not hot enough, the vegetables will become soft and watery. Sauté the vegetables over high heat, stirring and mixing very often. You may cover the skillet, but stir often to permit even cooking. When the vegetables turn bright green add salt or monosodium glutamate. Maintain high heat and cook until done. This whole procedure should take about 5 to 8 minutes, depending on the vegetable.

When vegetables are to be mixed with meat or fish, as is often the case in Chinese dishes, sauté the meat first, then cook the vegetables in the juice of the meat. This procedure is recommended because meat and vegetables must be cooked under different conditions. Meat must be sautéed quickly in a little oil and no water; vegetables may be cooked in a little water for a longer period of time. If you add both to the skillet at the same time, the juice of the vegetables will toughen the meat. Sauté the meat until three-quarters done, then remove it from the skillet and set aside in a dish. Leave the juice of the meat behind and add the vegetables, maintaining high heat. Cook the vegetables over high heat until almost done.

Stir frequently to permit even cooking. Add salt and monosodium glutamate if desired. Add the meat, mix and stir.

When cooking for guests, it may often be convenient to parboil the vegetables before sautéing. This will decrease the time of cooking by a few minutes. Wash and cut the vegetables as usual. Have ready plenty of boiling water and drop in the vegetables when the water is boiling rapidly. Remove the vegetables when they are bright green, drain immediately into a sieve or colander and run cold water over them. Drain the vegetables thoroughly. Sauté as directed.

Salad oil or shortening is recommended for cooking vegetables. Unlike butter these fats hold the heat better; hence will cook a vegetable much faster than butter will. You may use bacon fat also, to vary the taste occasionally.

Chicken fat is also suitable for sautéing vegetables, being light and agreeable in flavor. It may be used as a substitute for ordinary cooking fats and oils.

BASIC RULES FOR VEGETABLES.

In China, vegetables are almost never simply boiled in water. A little oil, a very hot skillet and some seasoning are usually all that is required to make a vegetable tasteful. The timing, the heat and the amount of oil used are of course dependent on the texture and the flavor of the vegetable.

In general it is possible to divide vegetables into five groups. You will find that since all vegetables in one group have more or less the same texture, they may be sautéed by the same rule. Group 1 takes the least time to cook; Group 5 the longest.

1. These crisp vegetables should never be permitted to become soft and soggy:

asparagus
celery
onions
green peppers
string beans
snow peas (peas-in-the-pod)
bamboo shoots

2. Leafy vegetables are at their best when served half tender and half crisp. Their flavor is brought out by cooking rapidly in oil and seasoning with salt.

Chinese cabbage
lettuce
spinach
leafy vegetables
bean sprouts
watercress

3. The following tend to become watery when cooked:

cucumbers
okra
tomatoes
yellow squash
zucchini

4. Cook these two vegetables as you would mushrooms. Use a liberal amount of oil and some soy sauce.

eggplant
turnips

5. These require the addition of a small amount of water to make them tender:

broccoli
Brussels sprouts

cabbage
carrots
cauliflower
corn

1. BASIC RULE FOR SAUTÉING ASPARAGUS, CELERY, ONIONS, PEPPERS, STRING BEANS, SNOW PEAS, AND BAMBOO SHOOTS (4)

Wash and drain the vegetable thoroughly.

Cut on the diagonal asparagus, celery, string beans or snow peas into 1½-inch lengths.

Place your knife at an angle to the length of the vegetable, to expose as much of the vegetable as possible.

Bamboo shoots are slivered or sliced thin, while onions, peppers are cut into rings.

For

3 cups vegetable

use

2 tablespoons oil

Heat the oil in a skillet. When the skillet is extremely hot add the vegetable. Maintain high heat. Stir frequently. Add

½ teaspoon salt
½ teaspoon monosodium glutamate (optional)

The skillet may be covered for a few minutes, but stir often. The time required for sautéing these vegetables should be about 3 to 5 minutes. The color should be clear; the texture crisp and tender. Serve immediately if possible; at any rate remove the vegetable from heat when it has reached this stage.

2. BASIC RULE FOR SAUTÉING CHINESE CABBAGE, LETTUCE, SPINACH, LEAFY

VEGETABLES, BEAN SPROUTS, WATERCRESS (2 or 3)

Wash and drain the vegetable *thoroughly.* Vegetables with edible stalks, such as Chinese cabbage, should be cut into 1½-inch sections. Break spinach, lettuce into pieces about 2½-inches long. The root ends of bean sprouts should be broken off, but since this is a tiresome job the tips are often left on. The tough stalks of watercress should be cut off.

Heat

2½ tablespoons oil for 4 cups vegetable

in a skillet until very hot, then add the vegetable. Maintain high heat throughout. Stir constantly but gently, seasoning with

½ teaspoon salt

Sauté the vegetables for 5 to 7 minutes, except for lettuce and watercress (2-3 minutes will do for those two). Remove from heat when the stalks are partly tender and the leaves a dark green.

3. BASIC RULE FOR CUCUMBERS, OKRA, TOMATOES, YELLOW SQUASH, ZUCCHINI (2)

Peel squash, cucumbers and zucchini. Wash and drain.

Tomatoes may be cut into wedges, but not peeled. Cut cucumbers, okra, squash or zucchini into ¼-inch-thick rounds.

For

2 cups vegetable

heat in a skillet

1 tablespoon oil

Add the vegetable. Stir gently from time to time. Season with

¼ teaspoon salt
pepper

Cook over moderate heat for 8 to 10 minutes. The skillet may be covered or uncovered.

4. BASIC RULE FOR SAUTÉING EGGPLANT, TURNIPS (4)

Peel the turnips and wash; drain. Wash the eggplant. Cut eggplant, peeled or unpeeled, into 1-inch cubes or into slices. Cut turnips into slivers.

For

3 cups eggplant cubes, or 2 cups slivered turnips

heat in a skillet

4 tablespoons oil
1 teaspoon slivered fresh ginger (optional)

The skillet must be very hot. Add vegetable and stir immediately. Maintain fairly high heat. When you are sure that the vegetable will not burn, cover the skillet. Permit the vegetable to become moist. Then add

1 tablespoon soy sauce, or ½ teaspoon salt

Cook covered, stirring gently from time to time. Cook for about 13 minutes in all.

5. BASIC RULE FOR SAUTÉING BROCCOLI, BRUSSELS SPROUTS, CABBAGE, CARROTS, CAULIFLOWER, CORN (4)

Wash and drain the vegetable. Cut the sprouts in half, if they seem tough. Cut corn off the cob. Peel the stems of broccoli; cut on the diagonal into 1-inch sections; slice each floweret into 2 or 3 pieces according to the size. Cut cauliflower into flowerets and cut each floweret in half. Cabbage and carrots should be sliced thin, as for cole slaw.

For about

3 cups vegetable

heat

1½ to 2 tablespoons oil

When the skillet is very hot add the vegetable all at once and sauté.

Cover the skillet. After a few minutes add

2 to 3 tablespoons water
½ teaspoon salt

Cook the vegetable covered for 10 minutes. If the vegetable becomes dry add a little more water.

COOKING WITH FROZEN VEGETABLES

Thaw completely and separate the pieces

1 box frozen vegetable

Drain off the excess moisture on absorbent paper. Heat in a skillet the required amount of shortening. You may use butter if the vegetable is served in an American meal. Sauté the vegetable in a moderately hot skillet. Use the seasonings specified. In addition, after 2 or 3 minutes, add

½ teaspoon monosodium glutamate

Cook covered, stirring occasionally to get even cooking. Follow the tables for *approximate* cooking times.

2-3 minutes

asparagus
celery
green peas
kale
spinach
string beans

4-5 minutes

lima beans
carrots

mixed vegetables
okra
Swiss chard

6-8 minutes

broccoli
cabbage
cauliflower
corn
Brussels sprouts

Frozen vegetables tend to hold more water than fresh vegetables which have been washed and well drained. Try to remove as much moisture as possible before cooking. Their flavors often are subdued, so they must be given an extra shot of seasoning (such as monosodium glutamate).

RULE FOR PREPARING CHINESE MUSHROOMS

Rinse the dried mushrooms several times in cold water and soak for at least 15 minutes in water to cover. Drain, setting aside the liquid. Cut the mushrooms in half or sliver them. Carry on as you would with American mushrooms. Use the mushroom water in place of any liquid called for.

Store the dried mushrooms uncovered in a glass jar, in a light place.

MUSHROOMS AND CHINESE CABBAGE (4)

Prepare and cut in half
1½ cups mushrooms

Wash, and cut into 2-inch sections

1 small head Chinese cabbage

Heat in a skillet

2 tablespoons oil

Sauté the cabbage in the oil over moderate heat for 2 to 3 minutes, then add the mushrooms. Season with

¼ teaspoon salt
½ teaspoon monosodium glutamate

Add a little water if necessary. Cook for about 10 minutes covered, or until the mushrooms are tender. Make the dish creamy by stirring in

2 tablespoons corn starch dissolved in ½ cup water

Use either Chinese or American mushrooms. This is very easy to make since the basic ingredients are both well flavored.

MUSTARD GREENS WITH MEAT SAUCE (4)

Grind or chop fine

½ lb. pork

Sauté the pork for about 5 minutes with

1½ tablespoons oil
1 teaspoon chopped onion or 1 clove garlic, crushed

Season the pork with

1 tablespoon soy sauce, or ½ teaspoon salt

Thicken the sauce with

2 tablespoons corn starch dissolved in ¾ cup water

Cook until the starchy taste is gone and the sauce is smooth. Wash and separate into stalks, or cut into 2-inch sections

1½ lbs. mustard greens (enough to make 4 cups stalks)

Drop them into a large quantity of

boiling water

Boil the vegetable uncovered for about 3 minutes. Drain immediately. Transfer the vegetable to a serving plate and pour the meat sauce over it, or cook the vegetable for 2 more minutes in the meat sauce.
The greens should be vivid in color.

This dish looks beautiful because of the jade-green color of the vegetable. It is also extremely tasty, owing partly to the very faint bitter flavor of the greens.

GARLIC SPINACH (3)

Wash thoroughly

1½ lbs. spinach

Drop the spinach into

2 quarts boiling water

Boil for 2 minutes only. Drain at once and run cold water over spinach. Drain again. Heat in a skillet

2 tablespoons oil
4 cloves garlic, crushed

When the garlic is brown and the skillet very hot, add the spinach. Maintain high heat. Add

½ teaspoon salt

Stir constantly. Cook the vegetable for no more than 3 or 4 minutes.
When it is almost done add

1 teaspoon sugar

Mix gently.

If you like garlic, you will love this. The spinach is parboiled to make it less watery and acrid. A little *sugar also helps to counteract the acrid taste; by no means should the spinach actually taste sweet.*

SPINACH AND MUSHROOMS (4)

Wash and slice very thin

1 cup mushrooms

Wash

1½ lbs. spinach

Plunge the spinach into

2 quarts boiling water

After 2 minutes, drain, and run cold water over spinach.
Brown

2 cloves crushed garlic

in

3 tablespoons oil

Add the mushrooms. Season with

½ teaspoon salt

When the mushrooms are moist and tender, add the spinach. Stir over high heat, seasoning with

1 teaspoon sugar

Cook until the spinach is barely soft, still a rich green.

MIXED VEGETABLES (4)

Wash and drain

1 small head lettuce
2 tomatoes

1 cucumber
1 zucchini
2 stalks scallions
2 green peppers

Cut the vegetables as directed in the preceding recipes. Heat in a skillet

2 tablespoons oil
the scallions, chopped

Permit the skillet to become very hot before adding the cucumbers, peppers, tomatoes and zucchini. Put aside the lettuce. Season the vegetables with

½ teaspoon salt

Maintain high heat and cover the skillet. After about 3 minutes, add the lettuce. Cover. When the cucumber is tender, the dish is done.

The ingredients of this dish are those of an American salad. The result is quite as interesting and delicious as any of the more exotic dishes.

EGGPLANT WITH GARLIC (4)

Prepare by Basic Rule No. 4 for

sautéed eggplant (see page 122)

Substitute for ginger

3 cloves garlic, crushed

Increase the soy sauce to

1½ tablespoons soy sauce

This makes a savory, rich dish.

EGGPLANT, TOMATOES, AND BACON (4)

Peel

5 tomatoes
1 medium-sized eggplant

Cut the tomatoes into quarters and the eggplant into 1-inch cubes.

Crush or chop fine

6 cloves garlic

Cut into 2-inch strips

6 strips bacon

Fry the bacon until it is light brown. Add the garlic and brown. Then add the eggplant, cover the skillet and cook for about 5 minutes, stirring occasionally. When the eggplant has begun to soften, add the tomatoes. Mix, reduce the heat and cook covered for another 10 minutes or so, until the eggplant is just tender and not mushy. Season liberally with

salt
pepper

Eggplant is at its best when the outside is soft, but the inside is firm. Stop cooking this dish when the eggplant cubes have reached that stage; otherwise this mixture will have no "body" and the whole will be too mushy and uninteresting. This is highly recommended for its successful blending of flavors.

CREAMED CHINESE CABBAGE (4)

Wash, and cut into quarters lengthwise

1¼ lbs. Chinese cabbage

Cut the quarters crosswise into sections 2½ inches long. Melt in a skillet

⅓ cup chicken fat

Add the cabbage when the skillet is fairly hot. Cook, covered, 10 minutes, stirring occasionally. Season with

¾ teaspoon salt

Use moderate heat so that the cabbage does not burn. When the vegetable is tender, stir in

1 cup milk, in which is dissolved 2 tablespoons corn starch
1 teaspoon monosodium glutamate

Cook until the mixture thickens and the starchy taste is gone.

Milk is rarely called for in Chinese recipes. This is one in which it is used to advantage, to set off the fresh sweet taste of the cabbage. The cabbage is sautéed longer than usual, because a rather tender quality is desirable in this creamy dish.

MARINATED RADISHES (2)

Wash

about 20 radishes

Cut off the green tops and crush the radishes, or slice them. Cut into slivers

1 green pepper (optional)

Marinate in the following mixture

1½ tablespoons soy sauce
2 tablespoons vinegar
1½ tablespoons sugar

Chill thoroughly before serving.

MARINATED CUCUMBER (2)

Peel, wash and cut into slivers

1 cucumber

Marinate and serve in this dressing:

3 tablespoons vinegar
1 tablespoon sugar
½ teaspoon salt

Chill before serving.

MARINATED TURNIPS (2)

Peel, wash and cut into slivers

1 turnip

Marinate in

3 tablespoons vinegar
2 tablespoons sugar
½ tablespoon salt

Chill thoroughly for about 2 hours.

These three recipes for marinated vegetables make excellent side dishes. They will stimulate the appetite, and offer a refreshing contrast with the rich foods of an elaborate dinner. You may also use them as part of the hors d'oeuvres, as a garnish for roast pork, cold chicken or canned abalone, sliced very thin. They would also go well with barbecued spareribs.

9
Seasonings and Sauces

EVERY SEASONING or sauce mentioned in this book is described below. In my own cooking I hardly ever use more than soy sauce, salt, pepper and monosodium glutamate as seasoning. I like the flavor of the original food to remain, unmasked by any foreign taste. The best cooks use seasonings judiciously and rely on buying ingredients at the height of their season, when the flavor is at its best, to supply the main quality of each dish. People who rely too much on prepared sauces in their cooking produce meals that are lacking in subtlety and good taste. This is, of course, a sign of poor technique.

All seasonings used in this book fall more or less into the following groups, and members of each group are to a certain extent interchangeable.

1. Onions, Garlic and Related Flavors
2. Salt, Pepper, Monosodium Glutamate, Soy Sauce
3. Cooking Wines and Liquors
4. Prepared Sauces
5. Chinese Condiments

1. *White Onions* are suitable for soups and stews. They are milder than yellow onions.

Yellow Onions, usually sliced, are used in braised and sautéed dishes. Brown them in oil to extract the flavor. It is the extract which counteracts any raw taste in the meat or fish.

Scallions are a small thin green plant with an onion-like odor. More delicate than onions, scallions are suitable for seasoning mild foods such as fish and vegetables.

Leeks are rather like large scallions. In France they are considered a vegetable. Be sure to split leeks down the middle and rinse out the inside as leeks often contain a bit of earth. Sauté to extract the flavor.

Garlic must be peeled and crushed, or chopped fine. It must be cooked with oil if it is going to flavor anything.

Ginger is a root sold in Chinese groceries. It looks like a highly distorted potato. Keep in a cool and dry place, as for potatoes. This is a highly pungent and biting ingredient. Sauté in oil, or use for soups. Most effective in combating gamy tastes. To make 1 teaspoon chopped or slivered ginger, cut a few very thin slices off one of the bulbs, chop or sliver. Do not peel the ginger.

Ginger tea is very good for upset stomachs and is made by boiling together for 10 minutes, covered, 2 cups water, ¼ cup sliced ginger, 4 tablespoons brown sugar. Add more sugar if the drink is too biting. Remove the ginger slices and serve very hot.

American Parsley. Very decorative.

Chinese Parsley. Wash. Use only the leaves, discarding the tough stems. Do not chop this parsley. Separate the leaves and place on soups, roasts, main dishes. This has a delightful fragrance.

2. *Salt*. When doubling a recipe or cutting it in half, don't change the quantity of salt proportionately. It will not work. Salt has to be present in a certain amount before it can be tasted. If you cut ½ teaspoon salt by half, the ¼ teaspoon salt may not be tasted at all. This is known as a threshold requirement. Furthermore, if you are doubling the number of portions, don't use twice ½ teaspoon as it will be too much. Taste as you go along if you are unsure. After a few trials it will come to you. And remember less salt is needed if Soy Sauce is to be added.

White Pepper is simply hot without having the aroma of black pepper.

Black Pepper is more spicy than the white variety.

Salt-and-Pepper-Mix is a very handy thing to have around.

Heat in a small skillet ¼ cup salt and 2 teaspoons white pepper.

Mix these ingredients over a moderate flame for about 5 minutes.

Cool and store in a salt shaker.

This can be used in cooking, but its main use is for seasoning fried foods (Fried Squab, see page 109; Shrimp Balls, see page 56). Roasts and broiled meats improve in flavor when seasoned with this.

Monosodium Glutamate is a marvelous discovery which has recently been introduced to America from the Orient. In the United States, it is sold under such trade-mark names as Accent, Enhance. Unlike salt or sugar it has no individual or original taste, but it enhances the flavor of the food it seasons. It dissolves in hot or cold water. This will do much to restore the taste of frozen foods, or foods otherwise altered by new methods of packaging. Monosodium glutamate is a breakdown product of proteins and is present in sizable amounts in soy sauce.

Soy Sauce contains both salt and monosodium glutamate; it is, therefore, a substitute for both those condiments. Soy sauce has been for years an ingredient of Worcestershire Sauce, but it has only recently come into its own in America. The soy sauces available at Chinese groceries are on the whole more full-bodied than those sold elsewhere.

The Chinese way of making soy sauce is to boil soybeans, mix the beans with roasted wheat and introduce a mold. Three kinds of mold may be used. When the molds have developed sufficiently, the mixture is placed in a salt solution, the pressed-out liquid is filtered, pasteurized and bottled. Besides the action of mold on the beans, bacteria and yeast also break down the soybeans.

Sugar is sometimes used in cooking main dishes. We often use it to combat saltiness. We have found that certain tastes may be modified by the presence of an opposite taste. To a certain extent the following rules are good and may be applied in an emergency:

too sour	add	salt
too salty	add	sugar and vinegar
cloying	add	salt
tasteless	add	monosodium glutamate

3. *Sherry* is most often used in cooking. It imparts a pleasant fragrance to meats and combats fishy and gamy odors.

Brandy is a suitable substitute for sherry, though more expensive. The addition of one teaspoon or more of brandy to a cup of hot chicken broth transforms it into a most nourishing and delicious soup.

Whiskey may be used also in the absence of sherry or brandy. I do not find its bouquet quite so satisfactory for cooking.

4. *Prepared Sauces*

Hot Sauce is made from small red hot peppers and is sold in bottles under that name. You may substitute *Tabasco* or *Chili Sauce* or any other sauce made from hot peppers.

Oyster Sauce is made in China. One method of preparing oysters is to cook and dry them. The dehydrated product may be stored indefinitely. Oyster Sauce is the extract of the cooked oysters; rich, slightly salty and having a fine bouquet, it is a complete sauce in itself and may be used over meats, vegetables, and some sea food. Use this sauce with discretion as one can have too much of a good thing. Available in Chinese groceries. The sauce does not taste a bit fishy.

5. *Chinese Condiments*

Sesame Seed Oil is a fragrant, aromatic oil which can be used to flavor soups and other dishes. The essence of sesame seed is concentrated in this liquid. A few drops in each cup of soup, or one or two teaspoons in a salad, will be sufficient to give a dish a lovely flavor.

Black Beans come in cans. These are very salty and have a pungent odor. You may or may not like them. Use sparingly, about 2 tablespoons to season 2 cups or more of food.

Bean Cheese or *Bean Cakes* are a kind of vegetable cheese, made from the fermentation of boiled soybeans and crushed rice or barley. The cakes are sold in jars in a semi-liquid form. The taste closely resembles that of Camembert cheese, being strong and pungent. This is a ready-to-eat condiment which is often served in a little dish along with salted peanuts, pickles, scrambled eggs, as accompaniments to congee, a gruel made of rice and water usually eaten at breakfast. The cheese may be used also in cooking fish, vegetables or transparent noodles. Use small quantities as it is strong and salty.

10

Rice and Noodles

BOILED CHINESE RICE (4)

Wash several times in cold water

2 cups rice (allow ½ cup uncooked rice per person)

After the last rinse leave enough water so that the rice comes up to about ¾ of the water level. Cover, bring almost to a boil. When the water starts to boil, stir once to loosen the grains from the bottom. Reduce the heat to low and cook covered until done. Do not stir the rice again. When the rice is cooked, the grains will be a milky white rather than a dead white, and each grain separate.

Allow about 15 minutes for 2 cups rice.

Rule for Storing Cooked Rice

Loosen and separate the grains with a pair of chopsticks or a wooden fork. Store in the refrigerator. When heated, each grain will be separate.

Rule for Heating Cooked Rice.

For

 2 cups cooked rice

add

 2 tablespoons water

Heat over a slow fire for 8 to 10 minutes. *Do not stir;* let the steam heat the rice.

RICE SCRAMBLED WITH EGGS (2)

Beat

 2 eggs
 1 tablespoon milk

Scramble the eggs. Set aside.

Heat in a skillet

 1 tablespoon oil

When the oil is very hot add

 2 cups cold cooked rice

If the skillet has not been well heated, the rice will stick to the bottom and become soft. Stir the rice over high heat until it is hard and grainy, seasoning with

salt, pepper to taste

Add the scrambled eggs. Cut the egg into the rice with the edge of a large spoon. Heat the mixture through. Sprinkle on top

1 teaspoon chopped parsley

A very pretty combination of white, yellow and green. If possible, use rice that has been stored overnight in the refrigerator.

PLAIN FRIED RICE (2)

Heat in a skillet

1 tablespoon oil

When the oil is very hot add

2 cups cold cooked rice

Stir often. After 2 minutes add

1 tablespoon or more soy sauce

Stir, mix until the rice is hard and grainy. Sprinkle the rice with some

black pepper

You can use this dish in place of potatoes in an American meal. It is much faster to make than, say, mashed potatoes, if cooked rice is on hand.

FRIED RICE (4)

Dice about 1 cup of any of the following cooked ingredients

sausages	lobster	bacon
meat	crabmeat	ham
poultry	vegetables	shrimp

For

3 cups cold cooked rice

heat in a skillet

2 tablespoons oil

Wait until the skillet is very hot; then add the rice. Stir. After a few minutes add

2 tablespoons or more soy sauce

Mix well. Add

the diced ingredients

Combine and heat the mixture through. If the mixture is too dry for your taste, you may add

1 tablespoon or more of juice, or gravy

To make fried rice successfully you should use cooked rice which has been left overnight in the refrigerator. This rice will not become sticky when fried and will give you the grainy quality which is desirable.

This is a good way of using leftovers. Be sure to drain any cooked vegetables before adding them to the other ingredients. You may add any leftover juice or gravy after *all the ingredients have been combined.*

FRIED RICE WITH VEGETABLES (4)

Method I (using cold cooked rice)

Cut into slivers

⅓ lb. pork

Chop

1 stalk scallions

Slice very thin

2 cups vegetables (cabbage, Chinese cabbage, turnips)

Sauté the scallions in

3 tablespoons oil

Brown them. Add the meat and sauté it, browning the slivers to extract the flavor. After 5 minutes or so, season with

2 tablespoons soy sauce

Permit the meat to absorb some of the sauce; then add the vegetables, cover and cook over moderate heat for about 5 minutes, until the vegetables are almost done. Add if necessary

2 to 3 tablespoons water

Add

3 cups cold cooked rice

Mix the ingredients gently; reduce the heat to low. Cover the skillet, but stir the mixture often to prevent burning. Add

1 to 2 tablespoons water

if necessary. The dish is done when the vegetables are cooked.

Method II (using freshly cooked rice)

Cook the rice (see page 138) for only 10 minutes after it has been brought to boiling. Follow the preceding recipe for combining the ingredients.

Heat the mixture until the rice is cooked and the vegetables are tender, about 10 minutes, over a low fire.

The idea is to finish cooking the rice in the juices of the vegetables and pork. This method makes it very flavorful. This dish is almost a meal in itself. If desired, serve cold cuts with it for a simple supper.

FRIED RICE WITH SHRIMP (4)

Shell, wash and dice

½ lb. fresh shrimp

Drain the shrimp thoroughly on a piece of absorbent paper. Beat and set aside

3 eggs

Chop fine

2 stalks scallions, or 1 small yellow onion

Brown the scallions or onions in

1 tablespoon oil

Add the diced shrimp and sauté over high heat for 3 minutes, sprinkling with

½ teaspoon salt

Pour the beaten eggs over the shrimp and scramble them briefly. Remove the contents of the skillet before the egg sets completely. Place in a dish and set aside. Clean the skillet and wipe dry. Place in it

1 tablespoon oil

Tip the skillet in all directions to coat it evenly. Use high heat and when the skillet is very hot add

3 cups cold cooked rice

Sauté quickly, using a "folding in" motion to get even cooking. Heat the rice thoroughly (about 3 minutes); now add the scrambled eggs and shrimp, using the edge of a large spoon to cut the eggs into the rice. Serve when hot.

This makes a very pretty dish, ideal for buffets as it may be kept warm on a chafing dish. I use fresh shrimp, as they are more tender and less salty than the canned ones, and well worth the extra trouble it takes to prepare them.

Rule for Preparing Parboiled Noodles

Boil

2 to 3 quarts water

Drop in

1 lb. noodles, or fine spaghetti

Cook for 4 to 10 minutes, depending on the thickness of the noodle. Test a strand by cutting or breaking it. The inside of the noodle should still be firm and hard, while the outside should be tender. Drain the noodles when they have reached this stage; rinse thoroughly with cold water and drain thoroughly. The cooking of the noodles will be completed when they are mixed with the other ingredients (see following recipes).

PLAIN NOODLES (6)

Prepare following the recipe on this page

4 cups parboiled noodles

Be sure they have been thoroughly drained (this is important).

Heat in a skillet

2 tablespoons oil

When the oil is hot add the noodles. Stir and mix gently. Bamboo chopsticks or a wooden fork is fine for handling noodles. Cover the skillet, but stir the noodles often.

Season with

1 teaspoon monosodium glutamate
1½ tablespoons soy sauce

Mix lightly and heat the mixture until all the liquid has been absorbed.

A simple but tasty method for preparing noodles.

I usually use the long thin Chinese noodles which are delicate yet firm. However, you can make this dish with macaroni or other kinds of noodles, the only requirement being that you drain them completely so that they will not stick to one another.

NOODLES, AMOY STYLE (7 or 8)

Prepare following the recipe on page 144

5 cups parboiled noodles

Cut into slivers

½ lb. pork

Wash, shell, remove sand and dice

1 lb. fresh shrimp

and dredge them with

1 tablespoon corn starch

Wash thoroughly

1 lb. spinach

Plunge the spinach into boiling water for 3 minutes, or until the spinach is bright green. Drain and rinse with cold water immediately.

When all the ingredients have been prepared, heat in a large skillet

2 tablespoons oil

Add and brown over a moderate flame

2 teaspoons chopped scallions, or 1 small chopped onion

Add the pork; when this is lightly browned, season with

1½ tablespoons soy sauce

Permit some of the liquid to evaporate. Turn the heat to high and add the shrimp. When the shrimp turn pink add

1 tablespoon sherry

After a few minutes season with

black pepper

½ teaspoon monosodium glutamate

Maintaining high heat, add the spinach. Cover, mixing gently from time to time. When the spinach becomes a rich dark green, remove all the ingredients from the skillet immediately, leaving the juices behind. Set aside the pork, shrimp and spinach.

Add to the juices

1 tablespoon oil

Bring the mixture to a boil and add the parboiled noodles. Handle the noodles gently, mixing no more than necessary. Cover and heat over a fairly slow fire. When the noodles are of the desired softness, add the pork, shrimp and spinach, mixing lightly and heating the dish through.

A favorite in our family. The specialty of our house.

SHRIMP AND ZUCCHINI NOODLES (4)

Shell and remove the sand from

¾ lb. shrimp

Wash, drain and dice them. Season with

½ teaspoon salt
¼ teaspoon pepper

Dredge them with

1½ tablespoons corn starch

Cut into ¼-inch rounds

3 zucchini

Prepare following the recipe on page 144 and set aside

2½ cups parboiled noodles

Sauté the shrimp lightly in

2 tablespoons oil

When the shrimp turn pink add immediately

1 tablespoon sherry

This will rid the shrimp of any unpleasant fishy taste. Allow the sherry to evaporate. Remove the shrimp and set aside; the shrimp need not be done at this point. Add the zucchini. Sauté it with

1 tablespoon oil
1 tablespoon soy sauce

When the zucchini begins to turn translucent, add the parboiled noodles and the shrimp. Mix gently; then cover and cook over moderate heat until the flavors are blended and the noodles are done, mixing gently with chopsticks or a wooden fork.

Light and not at all greasy, which makes it ideal for a summer dish.

11

Recipes Calling for Chinese Ingredients

PEOPLE WHO ENTER a Chinese grocery store for the first time are often struck by that peculiar, pungent odor which is a mixture of smells from the roast meats, pickled vegetables, dried fish and preserved meats which they see in bewildering array about them. Actually, what one does to these odd-looking ingredients to make them edible is quite simple.

The roast pork, basted all over with a delicious sauce, and the roast ducks and chickens, are, of course, ready to eat.

One cooks the leafy green vegetables more or less like American vegetables, according to the rules given in the previous section.

You will notice that many things are dried, such as beans, fish, mushrooms, dates, some vegetables. Soak these in water, rinse them several times, and carry on as you would with a fresh food.

As to pickled foods (pickled cabbage, salted duck, etc.) use them sparingly in combination with other ingredients.

It is possible to cook a very fine Chinese meal without any of these ingredients; however, for some dishes the real things are indispensable. Certain dishes peculiar to an occasion or place are seemingly incomplete without a specific ingredient, such as a kind of seaweed or a kind of glutinous rice. Then again, it is impossible to make "Sour and Hot" Soup without the bean curd and other ingredients which provide the textures, crisp and soft and smooth, to complement that highly seasoned soup. The Chinese stores are interesting because they have almost every edible, from pressed salted duck to shark's fins, for which there are no substitutes.

Why do we prize shark's fins? In the first place, because they are rare and must be brought from the South Seas; in the second place, eating them is a novelty. They are almost without taste. Cooking shark's fins is a challenge to the skill of the cook. The soup in which the fins are served must be just right. Its consistency must be creamy but not heavier than the fins themselves, for the fins should swirl and thicken the soup with their thickness. The flavor of the soup must be rich but not overdone, and should give off a definite but mild perfume. When cooked in such a soup, shark's fins are truly good.

Besides these expensive items, there are the relatively cheap ingredients such as dried scallops, dried mushrooms, tree fungus, bamboo shoots and tiger lilies. We eat these for their unique flavors and textures. Tree fungus, for instance, has an almost crunchy, gelatinous consistency not found in any other food. Its shape also is curious, resembling a twisted flower petal; furthermore, it is black and combines well with green snow peas and ivory colored shoots to make a dish a joy to look at and to eat.

Bamboo shoots are extremely fine as a food, being delicate in flavor, excellent in texture and pleasant in shape and color. We like them because of the very slight acid taste they give to meat and to mushrooms; the shoots also have a unique flavor of their own, which is brought out to a great extent by sautéing them with pork; for this reason these two are often found in combination.

Water chestnuts, seaweed, sausage, abalone, all these may be used for their interesting flavors, blended with the common ingredients which harmonize with them.

All these ingredients provide interest and are delightful to the palate, when their preparation has been careful. In the following dishes, as in the preceding recipes, it is important to work for a particular combination of flavors, to achieve an overall effect which is unique and pleasing.

WINTERMELON SOUP (6 to 8)

Scrub the outside of

1 wintermelon

Cut off the top and save it. Scoop out the seeds. Find a large deep dish or bowl which will serve as a base for the melon. Then find a very large pot into which the bowl and the melon will fit comfortably and may be lifted out without trouble. The pot should have a rack so that the melon will be above the water level.

Into the melon place

2 cups meat stock
¼ cup each diced ham, diced chicken breast, lotus seeds, mushrooms, Job's Tears
1 package herbs (called *ssewu,* optional)
1 teaspoon salt

Replace the top of the melon. Steam the melon for 3 or 4 hours, or until the pulp is almost translucent. The melon must retain its shape and should be firm enough to serve as container for the liquid in its cavity.

Dice very fine

⅛ lb. Chinese roast duck, or duck skin (optional)

Add this to the soup before serving. It adds another flavor to the soup.

This large green melon, which is flecked with silver, makes a clear soup, fine to serve with rich foods. You may cut up the melon into slices and make soup from the slices. A much more elegant way is to cut off the top of the melon and to scoop out the seeds and the spongy material surrounding the seeds. Into this place a little stock and the seasonings, and steam the whole melon for hours. The melon softens, the juices run out of the pulp and collect in the cavity, and there is a delicious soup! We serve the soup in the melon, carefully cutting out a slice of the melon itself to be placed in each cup, then ladling the soup over it.

TRIPE SOUP I (Beef Tripe) (4)

Scrub thoroughly, but do not cut

1 lb. beef tripe

Remove all the fat from the tripe. Place it in

1 quart cold water
4 slices fresh ginger
½ tablespoon salt
¼ teaspoon pepper

Bring to the boiling point, and simmer for ½ hour. Then add

1 lb. shank beef

Simmer for 2 hours or until the beef and the tripe are tender. Cut the tripe into strips with scissors, and the beef into chunks. Season the soup with

1 teaspoon monosodium glutamate

This makes a flavorful soup which may be served with noodles to make a main dish.

TRIPE SOUP II (Pork Tripe) (6)

Turn inside out and scrub with a stiff brush

1 whole pork tripe

Sprinkle generously with rock salt and rub thoroughly; rinse off the salt with cold water and the slippery coating should go with it. Repeat this procedure several times. Trim off the fat. Place in cold water to cover and bring to a boil; drain and discard the water.

Place the tripe in

1½ quarts cold water
1 teaspoon salt
4 slices fresh ginger

Simmer for ½ hour. Now add

3 pig's knuckles, or 1 spring chicken

The pig's knuckles should have been well scrubbed. Simmer for 1½ hours until the knuckles are tender and the meat pulls away from the bone, or until the tripe is tender. Skim off the fat and discard it. Season with

1 teaspoon monosodium glutamate

With scissors cut the tripe into pieces about 1 inch square. The tripe may be served separate hot or cold, or placed back in the soup. You may add

1½ cups transparent noodles (see page 162)

to the soup. Season with

½ teaspoon soy sauce to each cup
½ tablespoon brandy to each cup

More troublesome to prepare than beef tripe, but equally good.

BEAN CURD SOUP (4)

Dice or slice

1 or 2 cakes bean curd

Heat the curd in

3 cups soup, or consommé

Since the curd is made from cooked beans it is unnecessary to do more than heat it.

Bean curd is sold in cakes and will keep for about a week when stored in the refrigerator. It may be cooked as a vegetable, as a meat, or with sea food, and it can also be used to replace noodles or vermicelli in consommé. It is certainly a most versatile ingredient, since you may boil it, fry it, sauté it, steam it, or marinate it for salad. It blends well with other ingredients as its softness and blandness gives body to soups and complements the more flavorful foods and seasonings.

MUSTARD GREEN SOUP (4)

Wash thoroughly and cut into 1-inch sections

1 small head mustard green, enough to make 2½ cups cut vegetable

Add the vegetable to boiling stock. Use

3 cups meat stock, canned chicken broth, or meat stock substitute

5 minutes should be sufficient. Season with

½ teaspoon salt
⅛ teaspoon pepper
monosodium glutamate (optional)

On top of each serving place

2 small slices fine ham

Mustard green, like Chinese cabbage, makes a fine clear soup. It is a good light soup to serve at the end of a rich meal, or to precede one. Use the best ham you can find.

"SOUR AND HOT" SOUP (4)

Rinse thoroughly, and soak in water for a few minutes

¼ cup dried tree fungus
¼ cup dried tiger lilies (optional)
¼ cup dried Chinese mushrooms

Sliver

1 cake bean curd
the mushrooms

Heat these ingredients in

3 cups meat stock, or stock substitute

When the mushrooms are soft (about 5 minutes), thicken the soup with

2 tablespoons corn starch dissolved in ½ cup water

Season with

¾ teaspoon salt, or 1 tablespoon soy sauce
½ teaspoon black pepper, or 1 teaspoon Hot Sauce
1½ tablespoons vinegar

Beat together

1 egg
1 teaspoon water

Stir in the egg before serving.

Highly seasoned, this is a soup to whet one's appetite. In this recipe the tasteless ingredients, fungus and bean curd, are quite as important as the seasonings since they give the soup some body and their blandness serves to point up the hot liquid. This is a good soup to make in the summer as its piquant flavor will increase one's appetite as nothing else will.

SHARK'S FIN SOUP (4)

Shark's fins come dry, in sheets. Allow 2 sheets for 4 people. Rinse, and soak in cold water to cover

shark's fins

Change the water every ½ hour for about 2 hours, or until

the fins are soft. When they have reached this stage drop them into a large quantity of

boiling water

When the water again reaches the boiling point, drain and rinse under the cold water tap, until the fins are completely cold. Meanwhile, prepare chicken stock. Clean

1 large soup chicken

and place it in

1 quart cold water
3 slices fresh ginger
1½ teaspoons salt

Bring to the boiling point, and simmer very slowly for about 2 hours. Remove the chicken and the ginger slices. If there is too much fat in the soup, skim off most of it and save it for other dishes. Add the fins to the chicken stock and cook covered for about 1¼ hours over a *very low* fire. During this time the gelatinous material which makes up the fins partly dissolves into the stock, thickening it. When the fins are soft but still firm, they are ready to be eaten.

Sliver and chop fine

the chicken breast (enough to make ¾ cup chicken slivers)

Coat the chicken slightly with

1 teaspoon corn starch

This will give them a smooth coating, so that the chicken meat will not grate on the tongue. Chop

1 or 2 slices ham, enough to make ⅛ cup chopped ham

Stir

1 tablespoon corn starch into ½ cup water

Add this to the soup and cook for a few minutes, then add the ham and chicken meat. Simmer a few minutes more. Just before serving, stir in to make egg drops

1 egg white

With the soup also serve

vinegar
soy sauce

to be added to taste. About ½ teaspoon of each to 1 cup soup will improve the flavor.

This soup is a delicacy when properly cooked. What one must strive for is a rich soup, which is creamy in consistency but not in any sense greasy. It is flavored by the ham and chicken slivers, which blend to set off the gelatinous texture of the fins. The longest and thickest fins are the best, and are the most expensive. If you have bought good fins, do not try to save on the soup, since the fins must be cooked in a rich stock. An old chicken is best for soup, but its breast meat is, of course, not so tender.

ABALONE SOUP (4)

Cut

½ cup abalone slivers

Prepare also

⅓ cup ham slivers

Heat the juice of the abalone (there should be about ¾ cup) with

2½ cups water
¼ teaspoon black pepper

When the liquid is boiling, add the ham and abalone slivers. Add

2 cups watercress

or

1 cup mustard green sections

or

½ cup transparent noodles

Heat until the vegetable turns bright green, no more than 5 minutes.

Abalone is a shellfish which is strongly flavored and tastes like scallops. It is sold in cans. The fish itself may be eaten as it comes out of the can, or it may be cooked for a few minutes. The juice of the abalone makes a delicious soup, very easy to prepare and unusual in flavor.

SEAWEED SOUP (4)

Rinse several times in cold water

seaweed, about 8 inches square

Heat

1 can clear chicken broth and 1 can water

or

3 cups meat stock

or

3 cups water and ¼ cup dried shrimps

Add the seaweed and season with

¼ teaspoon or more black pepper

Beat

1 egg
1 tablespoon water

When the soup is boiling, pour in the egg and stir to make egg drops.

Seaweed comes dried, in sheets rather like tissue paper. It is purple and swells up when soaked in water. It makes a delicious soup, having that fresh tangy taste which we associate with all sea food. This soup is very easy to make and can be prepared in less than 10 minutes.

BIRD'S NEST SOUP (4)

Rinse repeatedly, then soak in a large bowl of cold water

3 whole bird's nests

or

1 cup bird's nests, loose

In about 3 hours, the tiny feathers should begin to separate from the jelly. With a pair of tweezers in one hand and a handful of the bird's nests in another, pick out the feathers one by one, and put the picked material into another large bowl of cold water. Repeat this procedure several times, or until most of the feathers have been removed. Prepare chicken stock as directed under Shark's Fin Soup (see page 155). Remove all fat from the stock. This soup should have no trace of grease in it. It is recommended for its "clean" taste, meaning that it is light and leaves the mouth feeling fresh. Cook the softened bird's nests in the

chicken soup

for about 15 minutes. Do not let the nests become too soft. Chop

1 or more slices ham

Sprinkle 1 teaspoon ham over each cup of soup.

This is even more troublesome to prepare than Shark's Fin Soup. Bird's nests, however, do have a distinctive, subtle flavor

that comes from a special kind of seaweed which the swifts eat prior to building their nests.

These swifts migrate yearly to the islands in the South Seas, where they build their nests among the cliffs and in the sea caves. Their nests are made of twigs and the edible portion, which is thought by some to be the "glue" which holds the twigs together, and by others to be food for the baby swifts. This gelatinous material forms a perfectly shaped coating on the nest itself, and is picked by the people of the islands who brave the snakes and slippery ledges of the sea caves to get this delicacy.

The first "nest" made by the parent swifts upon coming south is considered the best; the second one is not quite so good, for having been robbed of their first nest, the swifts must once again pool their energies to build a second nest. The third nest is the poorest, being thin and impure.

After these nests are picked, the bulk of the work still lies ahead. The tiny feathers and down must be picked out of the jelly-like stuff, and for this job a great deal of patience and many hours are required. The nests that one buys at a store have had the bulk of feathers picked out, but one always finds more when the nests are soaked and rinsed. Once this has been done, the care required in preparing Bird's Nest Soup is no more than that required for Shark's Fin Soup.

To serve either of these soups is a mark of great hospitality. No formal Chinese banquet is complete without one of these soups.

The nests are sold whole or broken; the former is the better quality.

SWEET BIRD'S NEST (6)

Clean and soak as directed under Bird's Nest Soup (see page 159)

bird's nests

Dissolve in water

rock sugar

Use about 3 cups syrup to 2 cups bird's nests. When the syrup is boiling, drop in the bird's nests and heat slowly for about 10 minutes. Serve hot.

Contrary to general practice, bird's nests are often prepared sweet in our native province of Fukien. We used to serve this dish as dessert at wedding feasts, or as the final course in a long and varied dinner. Since the above tastes not unlike Jello, and since bird's nests are so expensive, it is far wiser, we think, to cook it in chicken soup than in the above manner.

CHICKEN STUFFED WITH BIRD'S NEST (4)

Prepare according to the directions given under Bird's Nest Soup (page 159)

4 bird's nests

Clean

1 spring chicken

Stuff the body cavity with the bird's nests and close the opening with skewers. Place the chicken in a large bowl or in the top half of a large double boiler. Add

3 cups water
1 teaspoon salt
2 slices ginger

3 or 4 Chinese mushrooms (optional)
2 or 3 slices Virginia ham

Cover closely, place the bowl in a pan of water and steam for at least 1½ hours or until the chicken is tender and the area between the body and the drumsticks feels very soft and pliable.

An elaborate recipe which is well worth the trouble one takes to prepare it. The spongy bird's nests soak up the juices of the chicken, making each mouthful succulent. Since a spring chicken is used, its meat will still be soft and tender after steaming, while the small quantity of water used insures an excellent soup.

TRANSPARENT NOODLES

Soak the noodles in cold water. They will be soft enough to handle in ½ hour. Cut them in half with scissors if you think they are too long. Place them in boiling water, heat the water to boiling again, drain, discarding the water. Pour cold water over the noodles and drain. Place the noodles in hot

soup, or consommé

and heat for about 10 minutes.

These noodles are very light and do not have the starchy taste associated with vermicelli, macaroni, etc. Made from small green peas, they are sold in bunches, dry and white. They have to be soaked in water, and upon being cooked do become transparent. Very fine in size and almost tasteless, they must be cooked with something else to give them flavor. An excellent food for dieting people.

SAUTÉED TRANSPARENT NOODLES (4)

Soak in cold water for ½ hour

transparent noodles, enough to make 2½ cups soaked

Place the noodles in boiling water, heat them to the boiling point; drain and rinse with cold water immediately until the noodles are completely cold. This rinsing prevents the noodles from sticking. Drain thoroughly. Meanwhile, shell and remove the sand from

½ lb. shrimp

Dice the shrimp. Slice very thin

¼ lb. pork
¼ cup Chinese mushrooms, softened in water

Set aside the mushroom water. Chop

½ cup celery
1 yellow onion

Sauté the onion in

2 tablespoons oil

When the onions are brown, add the pork and sauté over high heat for 1 or 2 minutes; then add the diced shrimp and quickly sauté them. When they turn pink, add

1 tablespoon sherry

When some of the alcohol has evaporated, add

1 tablespoon soy sauce
black pepper (optional)

Add the celery and cook for about 2 more minutes. Add the mushroom water. Then add the transparent noodles, heat thoroughly. Note that the noodles will absorb some but not all of the liquid, unlike other noodles. For this reason the noodles are always less dry than wheat flour noodles.

The juices of the fragrant mushrooms, shrimps and pork are absorbed by the noodles. The celery adds another flavor to this

dish, and its crispness points up the slippery quality of the noodles. The dish should be delightfully fragrant, with flavors from each ingredient mingling with the others. It should be juicy and the noodles should almost slip down your throat.

STUFFED DUCK (4)

Scrub the inside of

1 large duck

with lukewarm water and 1 teaspoon soda. Wipe the outside, and singe off any remaining hairs by holding the duck over a free flame. Remove the glands on the tail. To remove the excess fat, first sear the duck. Heat a large skillet or put it in the oven at 400° F. If seared in the skillet, keep it covered but turn every 2 or 3 minutes to brown the duck evenly. Remove the melted fat as it comes off. When the duck is golden, remove it from the skillet or oven and drain on absorbent paper. Meanwhile, wash very thoroughly

1½ lbs. spinach

Drain until almost dry. Tear the spinach leaves in half. Chop or sliver

¾ cup bamboo shoots
¾ cup Chinese mushrooms

Sprinkle the body cavity with

¾ teaspoon salt

Stuff the duck with the spinach, shoots and mushrooms. Tie the wings and legs together and close the opening with skewers or by sewing the sides together. Place the duck in the upper half of a double boiler, or in a large stewing pot.

If steaming, add 2 cups water
if stewing, add 3½ cups water

Season the duck with

1½ teaspoons salt
5 slices fresh ginger

Steam for about 3 hours, until the duck is very soft. Stew for about the same amount of time.

Remove the excess fat.

Since spinach is acrid and duck tends to be rich and greasy, the two make a perfect combination which is neither too oily nor too sharp.

You may steam this or stew it. Use gentle heat to reduce the duck to tenderness. Steaming takes longer but produces better results since it cooks the duck more evenly and slowly.

CHICKEN IN OYSTER SAUCE (4)

Thaw (if needed) or clean

1 (1½-lb.) chicken, fresh or frozen
3 green peppers

Bone and dice the chicken or cut it up into small pieces. Dice the peppers.

Crush

2 cloves garlic

and brown it in a hot skillet with

2 tablespoons oil

When the pan is terribly hot, add the chicken all at once. Maintain very high heat and sauté the chicken. Sprinkle with

½ teaspoon black pepper

When the chicken is half done (3 minutes for diced chicken,

5 minutes for larger pieces) add

2 tablespoons Oyster Sauce

Mix lightly. Add the peppers and maintain high heat. Cover for a few minutes, adding if the ingredients are too dry

2 tablespoons water

When the peppers are bright green and still crisp, and the chicken is done, serve at once.

This is delicious mainly because of the Oyster Sauce. If you are working with frozen chicken, this is a good recipe to use since the sauce imparts a great deal of flavor to the meat. Thaw frozen meat completely before cooking.

CHICKEN WINGS STUFFED WITH HAM (3)

Clean thoroughly and singe to remove any hairs

1 lb. chicken wings

Cut each wing into two sections. Place the wings in enough water to cover. Do not use too much water. Simmer covered for ¾ to 1 hour, or until very tender. Cool. Slip the bones out and place in the cavity slivers of

ham (¼ lb.)

When ready to serve, reduce the liquid in which the wings have been stewed to 1¼ cups liquid. Add

1 teaspoon monosodium glutamate

½ teaspoon salt

Heat to boiling, thicken with

1½ tablespoons corn starch dissolved in ¼ cup water

Add

2 tablespoons port, or sherry

Heat the wings gently in the sauce.

This is sometimes served as one of the preliminary courses in a Chinese feast. It is troublesome to prepare but delicious, since chicken wings are considered the tenderest part of the bird, and the wings are covered with a delicate, creamy sauce.

SNOW PEAS WITH CHICKEN (4)

Clean

1 (2-lb.) spring chicken

Bone and dice it, or cut it up into small pieces. Dredge the chicken with

1 or 2 tablespoons corn starch

Sliver

2 slices fresh ginger

Wash

½ lb. snow peas (about 2 cups)

Break off the stems. If the pods seem too large and tough, cut each pod in half diagonally.

Heat the ginger in

3 tablespoons oil

Maintain high heat, and sauté the chicken in the oil. When the chicken is done (8 minutes), add

¾ teaspoon salt
½ teaspoon monosodium glutamate (optional)

Add the snow peas all at once and sauté for a few more minutes, maintaining high heat. Serve at once.

Remember to stop before the snow peas lose their crispness. What one must aim for is a velvety texture in the chicken, and a sweet, fresh taste in the snow peas.

CHICKEN STEAMED WITH SAUSAGE (4)

Clean

  1 (2-lb.) spring chicken

Bone the chicken if desired. Cut it up into small pieces. Dredge the chicken with

  3 tablespoons corn starch

Soak in a small quantity of water

  ½ cup Chinese mushrooms or more

Slice diagonally into 1½-inch pieces

  3 Chinese sausages
  ½ teaspoon salt

Find a deep dish which will fit comfortably into a large pot for steaming. Place the chicken, sausages and mushrooms in the dish and pour the mushroom liquor over it. To improve the flavor, add

  1 tablespoon whiskey, brandy or sherry

The sausage will provide all the seasoning that is needed. Steam for about ¾ hour, or until the chicken is done.

Chinese sausage is like saucisson *in its savoriness; waxy when cold, the lard becomes translucent when steamed or boiled. The sausage is very good eaten with rice. We often steam it by placing it on top of rice which is cooking.*

When chicken is steamed with sausage, the fat from the sausage melts and forms a layer on top. This layer of oil prevents any water from evaporating; hence the juices of the chicken and the pork from the sausages and the mushrooms collect and blend to form a wonderful gravy.

TIGER LILIES WITH CHICKEN (2)

Soak in cold water for 15 minutes

  1½ cups tiger lilies

The lilies will swell slightly. You may cook them with the chicken as they are, or make a loop in each flower to keep the fibers from separating.

Clean and chop into small pieces

  1 small chicken

Sliver

  2 slices fresh ginger

Sauté the chicken over high heat with the ginger in

  3 tablespoons hot fat

When the chicken is browned, add

  2 tablespoons soy sauce

Cook the chicken until almost tender, then add the lilies and cover. Reduce the heat to moderate. Add if desired

  2 tablespoons water

Cook for 8-10 minutes.

Most flowers are not edible, though jasmine and chrysanthemums are used to perfume tea. Tiger lilies have a slightly acid flavor and are quite palatable. Since these are flowers, they are very fragile. Handle them gently.

FRESH GINGER WITH BEEF (2)

Slice very thin

  1 piece ginger to make about ⅓ cup sliced ginger

Slice thin

  1 lb. steak

Heat in a skillet

3 tablespoons oil

Add the steak all at once, and stir immediately, maintaining high heat. Add the ginger about a minute after the beef. Stir frequently over high heat, for about 4 minutes. Add

2 tablespoons soy sauce or Oyster Sauce

When the steak is as well done as you like it, remove from heat and serve at once.

Fresh ginger is too hot to eat, but it does give beef a uniquely piquant flavor.

STEAMED SQUAB (1 Squab to each person)

Clean very thoroughly.

Be sure to clean out the body cavity, as well as the neck cavity. Singe any remaining hairs by holding the squab over a free flame. Soak in a small amount of cold water for 15 minutes:

Chinese mushrooms, ⅓ cup to each squab

Slice

⅓ cup bamboo shoots to each squab

When the mushrooms are somewhat soft, stuff the squabs with the shoots and the mushrooms. Fasten the opening with skewers or toothpicks. Place the squabs in a deep dish or bowl which will fit into a larger pan for steaming, or place it in the top half of a double boiler. Surround the squabs with

dried red dates

Pour over the squabs

1 tablespoon brandy or sherry to each squab

Sprinkle with

slivers of fresh ginger
salt to taste

Set the dish in boiling water, placing a piece of paper between pan and dish (see page 50) to prevent knocking. Steam for about 2 hours, adding more water to the pan as needed. The dates and the squabs should be so soft as to melt in the mouth.

Squab is very expensive but may well be worth the price when cooked the above way. This squab gives off a heady flavor, due partly to the brandy and partly to the dates. Rich and very nourishing.

FRIED BEAN CURD (4)

Drain on absorbent paper

4 cakes bean curd

Cut each cake into nine cubes. Fry in deep fat, a few cubes at a time, until golden brown. Drain on paper towels and serve hot. Make the following sauce:

1 teaspoon hot sauce
1 teaspoon sesame seed oil
1 tablespoon soy sauce
1 tablespoon peanut butter
2 tablespoons salad oil

Mix the ingredients together and place the sauce in a little dish for dunking.

Very simple to make and wonderful with cocktails. The texture of bean curd is altered by frying, the inside becoming juicy while the outside becomes crusty. Strongly recommended. The highly seasoned sauce is meant to give interest to this rather bland food.

BEAN CURD SALAD (2 or 3)

Place in boiling water for 3 minutes

2 cakes bean curd

When cool, sliver the curd. Soak

¼ cup dried shrimp (optional)

in

¼ cup water

Peel and remove the seeds from

1 large cucumber

Sliver the cucumber. Combine the bean curd, cucumber and shrimp lightly. If shrimp are omitted, sprinkle with

½ teaspoon salt

Season with

3 teaspoons vinegar
¼ teaspoon pepper
1 tablespoon sesame oil
2 tablespoons salad oil

Chill before serving. If desired, add to the salad

½ cup cooked chicken meat, cut into small pieces

Cool to look at and good to eat. You may try using a little sesame oil to flavor other salads; reduce the amount of salad oil by 1 teaspoon and use 1 teaspoon sesame oil.

PRESSED BEAN CURD

Place cakes of

bean curd

on a sheet of wax paper or cheesecloth stretched over a board. Cover with another sheet of paper, another board. Load the board with weights; a large pot filled with water or heavy books will do. Leave overnight. The water will be pressed out of the bean curd, making it more firmly packed and more easily handled when sautéed. Carry on as with any other vegetable.

Some people prefer the firmness of pressed curd.

SPINACH OR WATERCRESS WITH BEAN CHEESE (3)

Wash thoroughly and drain

1 lb. spinach, or watercress

Cut off the tough stems. In a very hot skillet containing

2 tablespoons oil

sauté the vegetable. When the leaves turn bright green, stir in

1 tablespoon bean cheese mixed with 1 tablespoon water

Heat thoroughly and serve.

For those who like bean cheese, as many do. This is very digestible, like all things cooked with bean cheese or black beans.

SEA BASS WITH BEAN CHEESE (4)

Cut into 1-inch cubes

2 cakes bean curd

Chop

2 stalks scallions

Clean

1 (1-to-1½-lb.) sea bass

Heat a skillet until very hot with

2 tablespoons oil

If the skillet is hot enough, the fish should not stick to the pan. Slightly brown both sides, then add the bean curd cubes and sauté them lightly. Add

the chopped scallions

½ cup water

Cover and cook over a low flame for about 5 minutes. Add and mix until smooth

2 tablespoons bean cheese

Cook covered until done, until the eye of the fish protrudes. This should take 15 to 25 minutes altogether, depending on the size of the fish.

This is very easy to make.

FISH WITH BLACK BEANS (4)

Clean and make 2 diagonal slashes on each side of

1 (1½-lb.) sea bass

Leave the head on, if only for decoration. Place the fish on a deep platter and sprinkle with

2 tablespoons oil, or 1½ tablespoons sesame seed oil (preferable)
1 tablespoon sherry

Chop

2 slices ginger
2 stalks scallions
2 tablespoons black beans

Sprinkle the fish with scallions, ginger and beans. Place the dish on a rack over boiling water, cover and steam for 20 minutes, or until the eye of the fish protrudes and the flesh of the fish separates from the bone.

Sea bass is best for this recipe. The blandness of the fish contrasts with the savory sauce. Black beans are highly flavored and have an interesting taste, rather like that of capers.

SAUTÉED ABALONE (4)

Prepare

1 cup abalone slices

Set aside

⅓ cup abalone juice

Prepare

¼ cup ham slivers
½ cup water chestnuts
½ cup sliced bamboo shoots
¾ cup snow peas
¾ cup Chinese cabbage (optional)
¼ cup sliced Chinese mushrooms (optional)

Heat in a skillet

2½ tablespoons oil
3 slices fresh ginger

Maintain high heat, add the bamboo shoots, Chinese cabbage and the snow peas. Sauté these for about 4 minutes; then add the mushrooms, water chestnuts. Cover and heat, reducing the heat to moderate. Add the ham and season with

1 teaspoon monosodium glutamate
½ teaspoon salt
¼ teaspoon pepper

When all the ingredients are very hot, add the abalone slices and juice. Heat for 2 or 3 minutes more and serve immediately.

If you are going to sauté abalone, do not cook it too long; otherwise the texture will be rubbery.

SAUTÉED SNAILS (2)

Crack the shells of

3 snails

with a hammer. Rinse off the snails and save only the ivory colored part. Dry the flesh and slice it as thin as you can. Prepare

½ cup bamboo shoots, sliced

or

1 cup Chinese cabbage, cut into 1-inch sections

Sliver

4 or 5 slices ginger

Heat the ginger in

3 tablespoons oil

Make sure the skillet is very hot before adding the snails. Stir the slices at once. Maintain high heat. The slices should curl slightly. Add

1 teaspoon monosodium glutamate
¾ teaspoon salt

When the snails are well coated with oil and begin to look cooked (about 2 minutes), add the bamboo shoots or cabbage. Keep on stirring. When the vegetable is done, add

½ tablespoon corn starch dissolved in a little water

and cook until the starch taste is gone. Serve at once.

These are not the garden variety of snails, or the escargots *one eats in France. They are the big snails that measure 3 or 4 inches across and are sold in Chinese grocery stores. In appearance they are like abalone or conch shells.*

Use the highest heat you have, add the snails all at once to produce an almost crunchy texture and to preserve their delicate flavor. You may have to practice sautéing these snails to achieve the right effect. Like kidneys, snails must be sliced very thin and quickly sautéed, to "surprise" them as it were. The same technique applies to both foods.

SHARK'S FIN OMELETTE (3)

Soak in cold water

1 cup shark's fins

Change the water every ½ hour for 2 hours. Drop the fins into a large quantity of boiling water, bring to a boil. Drain the fins and rinse under the cold water tap. Drain again. Prepare

½ cup bamboo shoots, slivered
½ cup ham, slivered

Beat

6 eggs

Heat in a skillet

2 tablespoons oil

Add the bamboo shoots and sauté them with

¼ teaspoon salt
½ teaspoon monosodium glutamate

Add the fins, and mix them gently with the shoots. Add the ham and heat the three ingredients through. Add the beaten eggs, mix gently over moderate heat until they are set. Serve immediately.

Surely one of the most elegant omelettes ever created.

TREE FUNGUS OMELETTE (2)

Soak in cold water for 15 minutes

⅛ cup dried fungus

Rinse the fungus several times and drain. Beat

4 eggs

Heat in a skillet

2 tablespoons oil

Add the tree fungus and sauté for about 3 minutes. Add

1 or 2 tablespoons more oil

and pour in the beaten eggs. Scramble till the eggs are set. Serve with a little

soy sauce, or Oyster Sauce

Very interesting.

SAUTEED PIKE WITH TREE FUNGUS (2)

Bone and skin

1 lb. pike

Cut the pike into thin slices. Dredge the slices lightly with

2 tablespoons flour

Soak in cold water for 15 minutes

⅛ cup tree fungus

Rinse thoroughly in several waters and drain. Slice thin

2 zucchini, or yellow squash

Chop

2 stalks scallions

Brown the scallions in

3 tablespoons oil

Maintain high heat, add the pike, and sauté until fish turns white; add the vegetables and the fungus and cover, mixing gently from time to time. Season with

1 teaspoon salt
½ teaspoon black pepper
1 teaspoon monosodium glutamate

When the vegetable is tender, serve at once.

The gelatinous, almost crunchy texture of the fungus sets off the bland smoothness of pike.

TREE FUNGUS SAUTEED WITH HOT PEPPERS (2)

Soak and rinse several times

⅛ cup dried tree fungus

Dice

1 large green pepper, or 2 small ones

Remove the seeds from

2 or 3 small hot red peppers

Dice the red peppers. Trim off the fat from

½ lb. pork

Dice the pork and dredge the cubes lightly with

    flour, or corn starch (optional)

Sauté the pork in

    2 tablespoons oil

with

    1 stalk scallion, chopped

Brown the pork, add

    2 tablespoons soy sauce

When some of the liquid has evaporated, add the tree fungus and mix gently. Then add the red and green peppers and sauté for a few minutes more. Taste the sauce. If it is not hot enough, add a few dashes of

    Hot Sauce, or Tabasco

A very pretty dish of black, red, green and brown.

SAUTÉED CAULIFLOWER (4)

Rinse and soak

    ¼ cup dried shrimps

in

    1 cup cold water

for 10 minutes.

Meanwhile, cut into flowerets

    1 small head cauliflower

Chop

    1 small onion

Brown the onion in

    2 tablespoons oil

Add the cauliflower and sauté for a few minutes. Next add the shrimp and the shrimp water, cover and reduce the heat. Simmer the cauliflower for about 10 minutes, or until barely tender. Thicken the juice to the desired consistency with

corn starch dissolved in water

Season if desired with

pepper
monosodium glutamate

This bland and rather uninteresting vegetable becomes palatable when cooked the above way.

TURNIPS AND SCALLOPS (4)

Rinse and soak in 1 cup water for 30 minutes

½ cup dried scallops

Peel

2 large turnips, or 3 small ones

Cut them up into chunks or small balls, using a baller. Place the scallops and the scallop water in a pot. Add

¼ teaspoon black pepper
½ teaspoon salt

Bring to the boiling point, reduce the heat and simmer until the scallops are tender, about 25 minutes. Add the turnips and cook for another 10 minutes. Before serving thicken the juice with

2 tablespoons corn starch dissolved in ¼ cup water

Stir in gently and cook until the floury taste is gone.

Make this with dried shrimp (soak for 10 minutes only) or dried scallops. Neither turnips nor scallops may sound very appetizing, but try this recipe and reserve your opinion until you have tasted it.

SALTED CHINESE CABBAGE (2)

Rinse under the cold water tap to remove some of the salt

2 stalks salted Chinese cabbage

Wring the leaves dry and cut each stalk lengthwise into 3 sections and then crosswise into ¼-inch pieces. Slice

½ lb. beef, or pork
1 small yellow onion

Brown the onion in

3 tablespoons oil

then brown the meat in the fat. Add the cabbage and sauté for 5 more minutes.

We like to add

1 teaspoon sugar

to counteract the saltiness. Sauté until the meat is done.

Cabbage is commonly pickled in China by packing it in brine. When cooked with a little meat, it is extremely appetizing. Serve this with rice.

SWEET AND SOUR CABBAGE (4)

Slice very thin, as for cole slaw

1 medium-sized head cabbage

Heat in a skillet

2 tablespoons oil

Add the cabbage when the skillet is moderately hot, sauté for about 3 minutes, then add

½ cup water

Cover and reduce the heat. Stir occasionally. Cook the cabbage until partly tender, about 10 minutes. Dissolve

2 tablespoons sugar
½ teaspoon salt

in

1½ tablespoons vinegar

Stir this into the cabbage.

One way of dressing up this common vegetable. Remember to serve this while the leaves are still a tender green.

SAUTÉED FRESH TRIPE (4)

Scrub thoroughly and remove the membrane from

1½ lbs. fresh honeycomb tripe

Wipe dry with paper towels. Cut the tripe with scissors into pieces ½ inch by 1½ inches. Heat in a large skillet over high heat

3 tablespoons oil
4 slices fresh ginger, or 1 large yellow onion, chopped

Brown the onion. When the oil looks terribly hot, add the tripe all at once and stir immediately, maintaining highest heat.

The slices should curl slightly. After a few minutes, add

1 tablespoon brandy, whiskey, or sherry

Permit some of the liquid to evaporate. Sprinkle with

1 teaspoon salt
¼ teaspoon pepper
1½ teaspoons monosodium glutamate

Cook for about 2 minutes more and serve immediately.

Use honeycomb tripe, and have the skillet as hot as possible before adding the tripe. When well prepared, tripe acquires a crunchy texture and a delicate flavor.

BITTER MELON (2)

Cut off the stem end of

2 bitter melons

Split them in half, and remove the seeds and the spongy material. Slice into ¼-inch sections, crosswise. Chop

1 stalk scallions

Slice very thin or sliver

½ lb. pork

Heat a skillet and sauté the scallions with

2 tablespoons oil

Add the pork and sauté quickly with

1 tablespoon soy sauce

When the pork is brown, add the sliced melons and stir, adding

1 or 2 tablespoons water if necessary

Cover, stirring occasionally. Season with

½ teaspoon salt

When each slice of melon looks somewhat translucent, remove from heat and serve.

Bitter, but with a sweet aftertaste; in this respect it is like some teas. This melon is probably at its best when cooked with pork or beef, tender on the outside but with a firm center. Some people like this very much, but others do not care for it. We find it quite delightful in the summer when the palate seems to need some kind of stimulation before one can really enjoy food.

SAUTÉED BAMBOO SHOOTS (3)

Drain

1 13 oz. can bamboo shoots

Discard the liquid in the can, since it has no flavor. Sliver the shoots. Cut into slivers

½ lb. pork

Heat in a skillet

3 tablespoons oil

When the skillet is very hot, add and brown

1 small yellow onion, chopped

Add the pork and brown it. Add

1½ tablespoons soy sauce

Permit some of the liquid to evaporate. Add the bamboo shoots, mix gently and cook covered or uncovered for about 10 more minutes, until the flavors have had a chance to blend.

Being the only vegetable which has neither leaf nor stalk, this vegetable is unique. Furthermore it has a delicate and delightful quality which is brought out by cooking it this way.

BAMBOO ROLL (4)

Cut into the finest possible slivers

2 cups bamboo shoots

½ cup soaked Chinese mushrooms

In a skillet heat

3 tablespoons oil

Add

½ lb. ground pork

and sauté it for about 5 minutes. Add the slivered shoots and mushrooms. Season the ingredients with

2 teaspoons soy sauce
½ teaspoon monosodium glutamate

Cook the ingredients over moderate heat for 5 more minutes, stirring and mixing constantly.

If desired, combine

¼ cup Chinese parsley

with the cooked pork mixture.

Cut 2 sheets of

strudel dough

into half lengthwise. Working quickly, place each sheet on a damp towel. Fill it with the pork mixture and roll it up tightly with the aid of the damp towel, as for strudel. Brush the top lightly with oil. Place the rolls on a greased baking sheet and bake them in the oven (400 deg.) for about 30 minutes, or until the tops are golden brown. With scissors cut each roll into 3 sections.

Strudel dough is available at specialty food shops. Its flaky texture is quite compatible with the delicate flavors of the filling. This makes an interesting first course.

FOUR FLAVORS (6)

Slice into pieces 1/16 in. thick, and then cut neatly into slivers 2 in. long, and 1/16 in. wide

Smoked sugar-cured ham (best quality), about ½ cup

Trim the slivers so that they will resemble a stack of matchsticks.

With a heavy blunt edge crack open the packing around

3 preserved eggs

Carefully shell the eggs, being careful not to break the "white." Rinse the shelled eggs and dry them gently. A mild odor of ammonia is to be expected. Cut the eggs lengthwise into quarters or eighths. The egg "white" should be translucent brown while the yolk should show concentric bands of greenish grey. The yolk may be runny like ripe Camembert.

Rinse and drain thoroughly

1 small bunch watercress

Remove the tough stems. Leave the cress unseasoned.

Using only the freshest

endive, 3 or 4 heads

discard the wilted outer leaves. Rinse and drain the hearts thoroughly. Cut the endive crosswise into 1½ in. sections. Toss it gently with the following mixture:

3 tablespoons oil
1 tablespoon vinegar
1 tablespoon soy sauce
1½ teaspoons Dijon mustard
2 cloves garlic, cut into large pieces

When the endive is to be placed on the serving platter drain away as much of the dressing as possible, and remove the garlic.

To serve, choose a large flat round platter (if possible one which is partitioned). Place in the center the endive in the shape of a small flat mound. Surround it with a thin border of cress. Place four stacks of ham symmetrically about the circle, and place the eggs between the stacks of ham. Place a little cress between the eggs and the ham. Carefully place over the eggs

a few drops of soy sauce
a sprinkling of very finely minced fresh ginger

To start a lengthy dinner it is convenient to serve a cold, easily prepared dish. This combination of complementary flavors is rather interesting. If one is exquisitely neat in pre-

paring this plate it can be most attractive. The dressing is also excellent with artichokes, cucumbers and cress.

FRIED MILK (BIRD'S NEST) (4)

Prepare

2 cups fried noodles (see page 220)

Arrange the noodles on a plate in the shape of a nest.

Prepare

1 tablespoon crabmeat, flaked
1 tablespoon minced ham

Beat until stiff

½ teaspoon salt
5 egg whites
½ teaspoon monosodium glutamate

Add

1 tablespoon cornstarch
¾ cup milk

Mix the ingredients thoroughly, then add the crabmeat and ham.

In a skillet which is not too large, heat

½ cup oil

When the oil is smoking, add the egg white mixture all at once and scramble the mixture quickly, for about 30 seconds. It is important to keep the egg white still fluffy. Place the mixture at once in the nest of noodles and bring it to the table.

This intriguing recipe comes from my second daughter. The result is quite extraordinary.

BRANDIED SCALLOPS (4)

Rinse, drain thoroughly and cut crosswise into halves

1 lb. scallops

Marinate them for 2 hours in

2 tablespoons brandy
¼ teaspoon pepper
½ teaspoon monosodium glutamate
⅛ teaspoon garlic powder
½ teaspoon salt

Beat together

2 eggs
½ teaspoon baking powder

Dip the scallops into the egg and fry them immediately in deep hot fat for 3 minutes. Drain them on paper towels and serve them while very hot. They may be kept hot in a moderate oven, but care should be taken that they do not become dry.

These are excellent with cocktails or as hot hors d'oeuvres.

CLAMS CANTONESE (6)

Clean thoroughly and place in a colander to drain

3 dozen hard shell clams

Prepare the following sauce: Sauté for 2 minutes

½ cup chopped scallions
½ tablespoon chopped fresh ginger
6 cloves garlic, minced or put through a press

in

4 tablespoons oil

Do not permit the garlic to burn. Blend in, away from heat,

4 tablespoons oyster sauce
1 tablespoon soy sauce

1 tablespoon sugar
2 tablespoons sherry

Dissolve and blend in

2½ tablespoons cornstarch
1 cup cold water

Stir the sauce over moderate heat until smooth and bubbling, and keep it hot.

Heat in a large pot or skillet with cover

4 tablespoons oil

When the oil is very hot, throw in the clams all at once. Stir with a wooden spoon. Cook the clams until their shells open part way, keeping the pot covered when not stirring. At this point, tip the pot to drain away the clam broth and add the prepared sauce. Give it a stir, cover the pot and cook just until the shells are all the way open. Serve immediately.

Choose small clams, which are daintier and more tender.

OYSTER MESS (4)

Place a colander or a large sieve in the sink. Bring to boil

2 quarts water

Into this place

1 pint shelled oysters

Immediately pour the contents through the colander, draining the oysters briefly. When cool enough to handle, cut each oyster into 3 pieces.

Combine

½ teaspoon salt
5 beaten eggs
3 tablespoons flour
1 teaspoon baking soda
¾ cup chopped scallions
½ teaspoon monosodium glutamate

Drain the cut oysters in a sieve and add them to the beaten eggs.

In a moderately large skillet heat until almost smoking

6 tablespoons oil

Add the oyster-egg mixture and scramble it quickly over high heat. Serve immediately on a large flat platter. Do not overcook.

SHRIMP ROLLS (6)

Clean and shell

1 lb. fresh shrimp

grind it with

½ cup pork fat
1 teaspoon salt
½ teaspoon monosodium glutamate

Combine it with

½ cup water chestnuts, drained
2 tablespoons chopped parsley
1 scallion, chopped fine
1 tablespoon sherry

Blend the ingredients thoroughly. Place a spoonful of the mixture in a piece of

wonton dough

Roll it up like a cigarette and seal it with

unbeaten egg white

Fry the rolls in deep fat until golden brown (about 4 minutes). Drain them on absorbent paper. To serve, stack the rolls on top of one another, like a pile of cigarettes. Garnish the plate with

radish roses
fried chicken giblets and livers (p. 100), using only ¼ the amounts stated

Wonton dough is easily obtained at Chinese grocery stores.

PINK AND WHITE SHRIMP (5)

Wash and shell

1½ lbs. fresh shrimp

Select small shrimp as they will be more tender. Larger shrimp should be cut into four or five pieces. Dredge them lightly with flour.

Combine and reserve

⅓ cup ketchup
1 teaspoon tabasco

Heat almost to the smoking point

¼ cup oil

Add all of the shrimp at once and immediately stir.

Add

½ teaspoon sesame seed oil
2 tablespoons sherry
1 teaspoon salt
½ teaspoon monosodium glutamate

The shrimp should be cooked in about 3 minutes. At this point, place exactly half of the shrimp on one half of a long platter. To the remainder add the ketchup mixture and heat through. Place it on the other half of the platter. Place a border of Chinese parsley between the red and the white shrimp and serve immediately.

This is an extremely simple and elegant dish.

DICED SHRIMP WITH CROUTONS (4)

Dice

2 slices stale bread

Fry them in

butter or oil

until golden brown. Drain them on paper and keep them in a dry place.

Shell and clean, and dice

1 lb. shrimp

Marinate them in

¼ teaspoon pepper
2 tablespoons sherry
1 tablespoon cornstarch
1 teaspoon sesame seed oil

Sauté them very quickly over high heat in

3 tablespoons oil
½ teaspoon salt
1 clove garlic, minced

The shrimps should be done in about 3 minutes. Add

1 teaspoon cornstarch dissolved in ½ cup water
½ teaspoon monosodium glutamate

Stir until the mixture is bubbling and smooth. Add the croutons, quickly mix the ingredients and serve immediately.

PIKE IN SEAWEED (6)

Tear up into pieces about 2 in. square sufficient

purple edible seaweed

to loosely fill one cup. Place the seaweed in

1 quart cold water

and rinse the softened sheets by repeatedly lifting them out of the water. Place the washed seaweed in a small pot and add

2 cups water
½ teaspoon black pepper
½ teaspoon salt

Bring these ingredients to a boil and simmer them for 5 minutes.

Clean, wash and dry

1 (3-4 lb.) pike

Make two deep slashes on each side of the fish running from top to bottom.
Wash and dry

2 leaves Chinese cabbage

The tough outer leaves with the sturdy stalks should be used. Place the fish between the two leaves, and tie them together securely at four points. Trim off the overlapping leaves at either end. Depending on the size of your skillet, leave the fish whole or cut it in half, leaves included.
Heat in the large skillet

oil to the depth of ½ in.

When the oil is very hot, place the fish in the fat and fry each side 10 to 15 minutes, with the skillet covered. Drain on absorbent paper, and when cool enough to handle, cut the string, discard the cabbage and transfer the fish to a plate. Place

4 stalks leeks cut into 1½ in. sections

in a large skillet with

¼ cup oil

and sauté them quickly without browning them. Place the fish in the skillet. Sprinkle it with

½ teaspoon salt
¾ teaspoon monosodium glutamate

Heat the fish for about 5 minutes over a moderately low flame. Meanwhile heat the seaweed and when this is boiling, pour it over the pike. Simmer, keeping the skillet covered, for about 10 minutes, basting the fish with the liquid to keep it moist.

Add to the skillet

2 tablespoons oyster sauce

mixing it well with the liquid. Add

2 tablespoons cornstarch dissolved in ½ cup water

When the sauce is thick, smooth and bubbling, lift out the

fish and place it on a deep platter. Pour the seaweed sauce over the fish. Garnish with

    Chinese parsley

and serve immediately.

This is an unusual dish in which the flavor of the seaweed sets off the firm, delicate flesh of pike. The cabbage leaves protect the fish during frying, prevents the fish from becoming too oily and makes turning the fish very easy.

STEAMED FRESH PIKE (4)

Clean and Sprinkle

    1 two-lb. whole pike

lightly with

    salt
    pepper

Place it in a lightly greased, shallow dish. Place the dish in a large skillet with cover or in a large pot. Place a piece of folded paper or foil between the dish and the skillet to prevent bumping. Add sufficient water to the skillet to cover the bottom but take care not to add too much or it will boil into the dish. Cover the skillet and steam the fish for 20 minutes, adding more boiling water to the skillet if necessary.

Meanwhile, heat together

    3 tablespoons soy sauce
    1 tablespoon gin
    ½ teaspoon sesame seed oil
    1 tablespoon sugar

Prepare

    ¼ cup finely chopped scallions

When the fish is done, sprinkle over it the chopped scallions. Over this pour the hot soy sauce mixture. Serve immediately.

This method of preparation produces superb results—but only if the pike is very fresh to start with. Do not attempt to make this with a fish that has been frozen.

FRUITS OF THE SEA (4)

1. Scrub well with a brush or a stainless steel pot cleaner

    1 lb. mussels or 1½ lbs. small clams

Be sure to remove the seaweed caught between the shells. Heat a large pot and lid over a hot flame. When the pot is quite hot throw in the mussels and cover the pot. After a minute, stir the mussels with a wooden spoon to permit even cooking. Continue to stir every minute or so until the shells just open, keeping the pot covered in the intervals. Remove the mussels from heat, collect the juice and reserve it. When the mussels are cool enough to handle shell them and pour the juice over the mussels to keep them moist.

2. Clean and shell, and devein

    ¾ lb. shrimp

Use small shrimp if available; if not cut each shrimp into two or three pieces. Dredge the shrimp with a small amount of flour and moisten with a little

    gin, sherry or whiskey

Gin is best for this purpose as it leaves little residual flavor.

3. Choose

    1 large or 2 small squid

Remove the tentacles by pulling them away from the body. These may be discarded entirely, or the ends may be cut off and prepared with the rest of the squid. Using scissors cut open the body, place it under the cold water tap and rinse away the gelatinous material, the bone, and remove any adhering membranes. Dry the squid with a clean cloth or a paper towel. Cut off the two flaps and place all the pieces flat on a dry board. Slash the squid diagonally in two directions, making diamond patterns about ¼ in. wide. Be sure not to slash too deep. Next cut the squid into pieces about ¾ in. by 1½ inches, lengthwise and crosswise to the diamond pattern. Place a colander or a large sieve in the sink. Prepare

1½ to 2 quarts of boiling water

Throw the squid into the boiling water, give it a stir and immediately pour them into the colander. Drain the squid well and transfer them to a bowl.

4. Clean, dry and cut into pieces ¾ in. by 1½ in.

½ lb. filet of sole or scallops

Blanch the sole as directed above for the squid. Place the blanched sole in a separate bowl. These four ingredients may be prepared in advance.

5. Prepare and reserve these for cooking with the seafood:

1 tablespoon chopped parsley (American)
¼ cup chopped scallions
1 teaspoon slivered ginger

Dissolve

1 tablespoon cornstarch

in

¼ cup water
½ cup milk

Heat these ingredients and stir them until smooth and bubbling. Add to the cream sauce

1 teaspoon monosodium glutamate
¾ teaspoon salt

Keep this sauce warm.

Heat in a large skillet

6 tablespoons oil

Add the parsley, ginger and scallions and sauté them briefly in a hot skillet. Do not permit the scallions to brown. Add the shrimp and sauté them quickly. Maintain high heat throughout the rest of this procedure. When the shrimp are almost done (about 3 minutes) add the sole and combine it gently with the rest of the ingredients. Add the squid after 2 minutes. Continue to stir the ingredients gently from time to time. About a minute after the addition of the squid, add

1 tablespoon gin

Allow a brief interval for the gin to boil away. Then add

3 tablespoons oyster sauce

Drain the mussels, discarding the excess juice. Add the mussels to the rest of the ingredients in the skillet, and mix them briefly. Cover the skillet and reduce the heat to moderate to permit the flavors to blend. Sprinkle the mixture with

½ teaspoon pepper
½ teaspoon monosodium glutamate

and add the hot cream sauce. Blend in gently and heat through. Serve immediately garnished with a lot of

Chinese parsley

Use fresh, not frozen shrimp. This lovely combination of foods is not difficult to prepare, complicated as it may sound. Remember that the flavors of seafood are delicate and that the ingredients must not be overcooked.

MARINATED SQUID (4)

Clean, dry and score

4 squid

It is very important in this dish to make the diamond pattern small, about ¼ in. wide or less. Cut the squid into pieces 1 in. by 2 inches. Bring to a boil

3 quarts water

When the water is rapidly boiling, throw in the squid all at once. The pieces will blanch and curl almost immediately. Drain the squid in a large sieve or colander at once.

Clean

1 large green pepper or 1 cup bean sprouts
1 stalk leeks

Cut the pepper into slivers. Drop them into a fresh quantity of boiling water and drain them immediately.

Combine the squid and the vegetables. Pour over them

2 tablespoons oil
1 tablespoon sherry
1 tablespoon soy sauce
1½ teaspoons vinegar

Blend the ingredients gently and briefly. Pour them into a serving dish and serve immediately.

The success of this dish lies in obtaining very fresh squid, and preserving its natural taste by rapid cooking.

FOOD OF THE FOREST (4)

Rinse with cold water and soak

⅛ cup tree fungus

Rinse briefly with cold water

½ cup tiger lilies

Soak them in water to cover. When they are soft make a loop in each flower to prevent them from separating.

Rinse and soak in water to barely cover

1 cup dried Chinese mushrooms (or use 1 cup drained canned button mushrooms)

When the soaked mushrooms are soft use scissors to cut away the tough stems which are discarded. If the mushrooms are about 2 inches wide, cut each one in half; if smaller, leave them whole.

Cut a gash on the flat side of

fresh chestnuts, sufficient to make about ½ cup

Drop them into boiling water and boil them for 5 minutes.

Do not drain the chestnuts as this will make peeling them more difficult. Shell the chestnuts and remove the membranes. Cut each nut in half.

Drain, discarding the water

1 (13 oz.) can bamboo shoots

Cut each piece lengthwise and then crosswise into slices about 1/16 in. thick and 1 in. wide.

Rinse and snap off the tough ends of

½ lb. asparagus,

Cut the asparagus diagonally into 1½ inch spears.

Sliver

1 small chunk ginger, to make about 1 tablespoonful

Heat in a moderately large skillet

3 tablespoons oil

Sauté the ginger briefly and add the mushrooms and chestnuts. Sauté these ingredients over moderate heat for about 2 minutes. Add the tree fungus and raise the heat slightly. Add

1 teaspoon monosodium glutamate
1 tablespoon soy sauce

and

a little canned chicken broth or meat stock

to keep the ingredients moist and juicy. Stir and mix to permit even cooking, adding more broth as needed. Cook the ingredients for 10 minutes in this fashion, remove them from the skillet and set them aside.

In the same skillet heat

3 tablespoons oil

Add the bamboo shoots and asparagus and sauté them for 3 minutes over moderate heat, adding

½ teaspoon salt

Remove the vegetables and set them aside.

Sauté the tiger lilies with

1 teaspoon oil
1 teaspoon soy sauce

for 3 minutes. Then add the mushrooms, chestnuts and fungus. Cover the skillet to permit the flavors to blend. Cook them with occasional stirring for about 5 minutes. Add the bamboo shoots and asparagus and add

1 teaspoon sugar

Heat the ingredients through and serve immediately.

BRAISED MUSHROOMS (4)

Rinse in cold water and soak in barely enough water to cover

2 cups Chinese mushrooms, dried

When the mushrooms have softened, cut off the tough stems. Leave the mushrooms whole, no matter what their size. Discard those that are broken or save them for some other dish. Simmer the mushrooms in the soaking water plus

1 can beef broth

for about 20 minutes. Add

1 teaspoon monosodium glutamate
1 tablespoon oyster sauce
1 teaspoon sherry

Dissolve in a small quantity of the broth

3 tablespoons cornstarch

and return this to the remainder. With a wooden spoon stir until the mixture is smooth. Place the mushrooms neatly in a fairly small deep dish, tops up, making a circular pattern. Over this pour enough of the sauce to cover the mound generously.

Of all the foods known the Chinese mushroom is perhaps the most delicious. This is rich, succulent and delicate. Choose large, thick Chinese mushrooms, which have curled edges.

LOHAN TSAI (FEAST OF ARAHATS) (5-6)

Prepare the nine ingredients as follows.

1. Winter melon. Remove any membranes and seeds and peel the melon. Slice it into pieces about 1½ inches square and ⅛ in. thick. Parboil 1 cup sliced melon in about 1 quart water. Drain the melon slices.
2. Bamboo shoots. Use half a 13 oz. can. Drain the shoots and slice them into 1/16 in. thick pieces.
3. Fa-ts'ai (a kind of seaweed resembling hair). Drop a small handful into boiling water, simmer them for a few minutes. Drain the seaweed and run cold water over it, draining it well again.
4. Tree fungus. Rinse 1½ tablespoonfuls with cold water. Soak it in 1 cup cold water and when it has swelled, drain it well.
5. Tiger lilies (chin-chen). Soften ¼ cup lilies in cold water. Make a loop in each flower to keep the fibers together during subsequent cooking, and cut off the hard stem.
6. Dried bean curd (toufu-p'i). Bring to a boil and simmer for 1 hour or more, sufficient quantity to make 1 cupful curd cut into 1 inch sections.
7. Gingko. Use ⅓ cup of the drained, canned fruit.
8. Water chestnuts. Prepare ½ cup canned chestnuts or an equivalent amount of the fresh peeled chestnuts. Slice crosswise into ⅛ inch slices.
9. Hearts of Chinese cabbage. Use only the most tender parts of the cabbage. Slice the hearts into 2 inch sections, to make 1½ cups.

Heat in a large, deep skillet

¼ cup oil

When the oil is very hot, add all the ingredients at once and sauté them quickly over high heat. Cook them for about 5 minutes, mixing and stirring them constantly. Then add

3 tablespoons soy sauce

Sauté the ingredients for about 2 more minutes, blending in the sauce.

Add

½ cup water

Reduce the heat and cover the skillet. Simmer the ingredients for 10 minutes, stirring occasionally. Add and cook for 10 more minutes

1 tablespoon medium or dark brown sugar

Add

½ teaspoon monosodium glutamate
¾ cup water

in which is dissolved

1 tablespoon cornstarch

to make a smooth sauce.

This interesting Buddhist dish derives its flavor mainly from the seaweed and the bamboo shoots. The bean curd gives the dish both body and flavor, while the lilies, gingko and tree fungus provide different textures. It is a kind of vegetarian stew.

LIONS' HEADS (4)

Grind together

2 slices fresh ginger
1¼ lbs. pork
¼ lb. pork fat

or use in all 1½ lbs. pork which is well larded.

Blend this with

2 tablespoons soy sauce
¼ cup flour
1 tablespoon water

Shape the meat into 4 or 5 large balls.

Wash and cut into 4 in. sections

1 medium head Chinese cabbage

Using half the cabbage, line the bottom and sides of an earthenware or iron casserole, or heavy pot. Place the meat balls in the center, and cover them with the remaining cabbage, packing in the sides well. Sprinkle the top with

½ teaspoon salt

Add

1½ cups meat stock, canned meat broth or water to which has been added ½ teaspoon monosodium glutamate

The liquid should come up to half the height of the casserole. Simmer the casserole on top of the stove or in a slow oven 275 deg. for 3 to 4 hours. Serve it in the same casserole.

The addition of flour to the meat keeps it juicy and holds in the soy sauce. Be sure to have a high proportion of fat in the meat mixture, to keep the balls light. The cabbage will absorb the fat, at the same time, making the soup flavorful. This dish is to be served with rice as a main course.

BEEF WITH ONIONS (2)

Rub

a ¾ lb. piece of steak

on both sides with

1 teaspoon baking soda.

Let the meat stand for 1 hour and then cut it into thin slices. Blend the meat with

½ teaspoon black pepper
1 tablespoon soy sauce
1 tablespoon flour

Slice into very thin rings

3 large yellow onions

Sauté them in

2 tablespoons oil
a little salt

until the rings become translucent but still retain their crispness. Remove the onion from the skillet and set it aside. Add to the skillet

1 teaspoon chopped black beans (toushi)
1 tablespoon oil

When the skillet is very hot add the meat and sauté it briefly (for 1-2 minutes). Add the onions, heat the ingredients through and serve immediately.

A commonplace dish which can be excellent if the beef remains somewhat underdone and the onions are sweet. The baking soda makes the meat tender.

ROAST VEAL, WITH MUSHROOMS (6)

Prepare and roast according to the Western fashion a

3 lb. veal roast

making sure that the veal has enough fat on it or added to it during roasting. Slivers of garlic should be placed deep inside the roast to flavor the meat during cooking. This may be done easily by plunging a sharp thin knife into the meat or along the bone and slipping in slivers of garlic as far as they will go. Sprinkle the roast with salt and pepper.

Meanwhile, rinse briefly with cold water

1½ cups dried Chinese mushrooms

and then soak them in water to cover. When they are soft,

cut away the hard stem and discard them. Cut the caps into thin slivers and replace them in the water. Bring the mushrooms to a boil in the water in which they have been soaked and simmer them for about 20 minutes.

Add

1 teaspoon monosodium glutamate
½ teaspoon salt

When the veal is done, add the drippings to the mushrooms and thicken the sauce with a little

cornstarch dissolved in water

The roast may be served in the Western fashion with the sauce as an accompaniment or carved, cubed and mixed with the mushrooms before serving.

Veal is rarely served in China. Nevertheless this combination which is not authentically Chinese, is too good to omit. The fragrance of Chinese mushrooms goes well with the delicacy of veal.

VEAL STEW WITH TENDONS (6)

Wash and dry thoroughly

12 dried calf's tendons

Fry the dried tendons in deep fat until they are curled and slightly browned. Drain the tendons on paper.

In a skillet heat

3 tablespoons oil

and sauté the following ingredients in it for 5 minutes

1 lb. veal, cut into 1½ in. cubes
½ lb. pork, cut into 1 in. cubes
2 whole white onions, peeled

Season the meat with

½ teaspoon salt

¼ teaspoon monosodium glutamate
¼ teaspoon white pepper

Add the fried tendons and

2 cups water

Bring the mixture to a boil. Then add

12 Chinese mushrooms, washed and soaked
½ cup sliced bamboo shoots

and simmer it for 2 hours, or until the tendons are tender. Add more water as needed.

Calf's tendons impart to the stew a creamy consistency. In themselves they are tasteless, so one must utilize the pork and mushrooms and shoots to give flavor to this dish.

TWICE-COOKED PORK (Huei-kuo-rou) (4)

A boned fresh ham or a piece of belly pork should be used for this recipe, which requires that the meat be part lean, part fat and part skin. The remainder of the ham may be stewed or roasted.

Cut off a

1 lb. piece of pork

Leave it whole. Place it in water to cover and simmer it for 45 minutes, or until very tender. Remove it from the stock. When cool, cut it into slices 1 in. by 2 inches, about ¼ in. thick.

Remove the seeds from

2 green peppers
1 red pepper
several small red hot peppers (optional)

Cut the peppers into coin size pieces, and dice the small hot peppers.

String

¼ lb. snow peas

Rinse and drain them.

Sauté the peppers for about 2 minutes in a very hot skillet with

1 tablespoon oil

Remove them from the skillet and set them aside. Sauté the snow peas for 1 minute in a very hot skillet with

¼ teaspoon salt
1½ tablespoons oil

Remove the peas from the skillet and set them aside.

To the skillet add

3 tablespoons oil

When the skillet is very hot add the pork slices. Sauté them over high heat, adding

1½ tablespoons Chinese barbecue sauce (hoi-sin sauce) mixed with 1 tablespoon water

Cook the pork for about 5 minutes. Add the peppers and cook for 2 more minutes. Add the snow peas and heat the mixture through.

A tasty dish which should always be served with rice, especially if the hot peppers are included.

THRICE-COOKED PORK (K'ou-rou) (4)

Clean and trim, but leave whole

a 1½ lb. piece of boned fresh ham, or belly pork.

Simmer it in water to cover for 1 hour or longer. Remove the meat from the stock. When cool, prick the skin with a fork and rub into it a small amount of

honey

Fry the boiled pork in deep fat, slowly, until the skin is a golden brown. Now place it in a shallow large dish containing

vinegar

Coat the meat on all sides with the vinegar, and let it stand for 10 minutes. Then place the meat in a large bowl of cold water for 30 minutes.

Peel

1 large piece of taro (yu-t'ou)

Cut it into slices ¼ in. thick and about 3 inches long and 1 in. wide. Fry the slices in deep fat until almost crusty. Remove the meat from the cold water and slice the meat approximately the same size as the taro. Place alternate layers of meat and taro in a heat proof deep dish. Sprinkle each layer with a mixture of

2 tablespoons soy sauce
1 tablespoon sherry
1 tablespoon brown sugar

Cover the dish closely with aluminum foil. Steam it for 2 hours or more. When ready to serve invert the dish on to a plate.

A most unusual dish which is at once rich and delicate. The pork should melt in one's mouth.

CRISPY-SKINNED PORK (6)

Rinse under the cold tap, and wipe dry

a 1½ lb. piece of belly pork

The pork should be relatively lean. Score the skin, making diamond patterns about ¾ in. wide. Broil the meat for about 20 minutes under a moderate flame, skin side up, or until it is brown. Remove the meat from the broiler and paint it with the following mixture on the meat side only.

1 tablespoon Chinese barbecue sauce (Hoi-sin sauce)
2 tablespoons brown sugar
3 tablespoons soy sauce

Place the meat, lean side up on a rack over a pan. Roast it in a 375 degree oven for about 45 minutes. When cool, chop the pork into pieces ½ in. by 1½ inches.

This dish is served cold, without sauce. It makes an unusual and tasty appetizer, or it may be served with cocktails.

SHREDDED PORK (Rou-sung)

Trim all the fat off

4 lbs. pork tenderloin

Cut the pork into 1¼ inch cubes. Place it in a pot and add

1 head of garlic, peeled and crushed to a paste
⅔ cup soy sauce
⅓ cup red bean curd (hung toufu-ru)
¾ cup water
3 tablespoons medium or dark brown sugar

Keep the pot covered as much as possible. Beginning with the stewing, this entire process is carried through using the lowest possible heat. The pork must be stewed with constant stirring so it does not burn. Simmer the stew for about 2 hours, until the pork is quite dry. During the course of the stewing, try to separate the fibers with a wooden spoon. When the liquid has evaporated, and some oil has collected at the bottom of the pot, and the fibers are falling apart, transfer the contents of the pot to a large skillet. Over constant very low heat, stir and separate the meat fibers with a wooden spoon. This process requires 1-2 more hours. The meat should resemble matted wool, taste very slightly toasted, be quite dry yet taste succulent. The important point is to keep heating, stirring and separating the fibers until they are very delicate and dry. When the fibers look wooly, you may stop. Place the meat on a large piece of brown paper or on several layers of paper towels, spreading it over a large area so that the fat will drain out. When the meat is absolutely cold place it in tins which you may seal with adhesive tape if they are not to be used right away. If the meat loses its crispness you may dry it again by placing it on a baking sheet in a 350 degree oven for about 15 min.

This method of preserving meat is time-consuming and tiring, but the result is unusual and delicious. Rou-sung may be served with congee, or as a snack. It is also extraordinarily good on a piece of buttered bread. This is also an Amoy recipe.

WINED CHICKEN WINGS (3)

Clean

12 chicken wings

Simmer them for 1 hour, or until tender, in

1 can beef or chicken broth
2 tablespoons sherry
½ teaspoon salt

When they are cool enough to handle, cut off the wing tips and discard them. Separate the upper and lower joints and, if desired, slip out the bones. Save the broth.

Heat until very hot

½ cup oil

Add the chicken wings at once and brown them. Add

2 cloves garlic, peeled and cut

When the wings are evenly browned and crisp, place them on a serving plate. Heat the broth in which the wings were simmered, adding

1 teaspoon soy sauce
½ teaspoon monosodium glutamate

Dissolve in a bit of the broth

1 tablespoon cornstarch

and return it to the remainder of the liquid. Stir until smooth and bubbling and pour it over the fried chicken. Garnish the dish with

Fried Parsley Sprigs

This entire procedure may be applied to a whole small chicken, but as I do not find this practicable since it requires a large cauldron of frying oil, it has been adapted to the present form. The result is excellent from the point of view of texture and taste.

CHICKEN STEWED WITH RED DATES (4)

Cut

a ½ lb. piece of bacon

into small chunks. If a whole piece of bacon is unobtainable use thick sliced bacon cut into 1 inch sections.
Clean thoroughly by slicing lengthwise and rinsing under the cold tap

1 large stalk leeks

Cut the leek crosswise into 1½ inch sections. Sauté the leek with the bacon. Add

1 2½ lb. chicken, cut into small pieces

Sauté the chicken in the bacon fat for about 7 minutes, turning the pieces often. Season the chicken with

1 tablespoon soy sauce or ½ teaspoon salt

Add

2 tablespoons sherry
¾ cup dried Chinese red dates, rinsed

Simmer the chicken, covered for 45 minutes to 1 hour, stirring occasionally.

Red dates impart a slightly acid, sweet taste to the chicken which is balanced by the richness of the bacon.

GAME HENS IN FOIL (allow one hen for each person)

Clean thoroughly

Rock Cornish Game Hens

Discard the insides. Dry the body cavity.

For each bird chop very fine or grind

2 strips bacon

Blend it with

1 teaspoon Chinese barbecue sauce (Hoi-sin Sauce)

Spread the bacon mixture evenly over the body cavity. Coat the birds on the outside with the following mixture

¼ cup soy sauce
½ cup Chinese barbecue sauce
¼ cup ketchup
2 tablespoons gin
1 tablespoon oil

Marinate the birds in the sauce for at least 2 hours. For each bird prepare a sheet of heavy aluminum foil 15 by 12 inches. Spread the foil in the center only with

lard

Drain excess sauce from the birds, and place skewers in them to close the cavity. Place the bird on the larded portion of the foil and cover the breast with

2 two-inch strips of bacon

Carefully fold the edges of the foil together to seal the bird completely, being careful not to break it. Place the birds well apart on a large baking sheet in a 400 degree oven for about 30-35 minutes. Serve the birds in the foil.

I find Rock Cornish Game Hens somewhat lacking in flavor. This recipe attempts to correct that defect.

MOCHA CHICKEN (4)

Clean and wipe dry

5 or 6 chicken legs

Separate the joints. Marinate them for 3 to 4 hours in the following mixture

⅔ cup soy sauce
½ cup brown sugar
¼ cup sherry
¼ cup very strong cold coffee
1 tablespoon oil

Drain the chicken pieces well. Sprinkle them with

black pepper

Heat in a skillet

2 tablespoons oil

Coat the skillet evenly with the oil. When it is very hot, add the chicken, and brown it quickly on all sides. Meanwhile, heat the soy sauce mixture in which the chicken was marinated. Pour it into the skillet. Simmer the chicken in the sauce for 20 to 25 minutes. Remove the pieces immediately and let them cool on a plate. When lukewarm or cold, chop up the pieces and serve them plain or with a little of the sauce.

This recipe was originally devised for cooking a whole chicken, but I find it better suited to cooking parts of chicken. Use only the best Chinese soy sauce.

WALNUT CHICKEN (4)

Chop coarsely and place under the broiler to toast

⅔ cup walnuts

Bone and skin

1 lb. chicken breasts

Cut the meat into coarse slivers about 1¼ inches long. Blend in by hand

1 egg white, unbeaten
1½ tablespoons cornstarch
½ teaspoon salt
¼ teaspoon monosodium glutamate

Sauté for 5 minutes

⅔ cup diced bamboo shoots

in

2 tablespoons oil
¼ teaspoon salt

Remove this from the skillet and reserve.

To the skillet add

3 tablespoons oil

When the oil approaches the smoking point add

2 cloves garlic, minced

and the chicken. Sauté the chicken over highest heat, mixing with a fork or chopsticks. When the meat has blanched add

1 teaspoon soy sauce
1 tablespoon sherry

Sauté the chicken for 2-3 minutes more. Add the bamboo shoots, heat the mixture through and add at the last moment the toasted walnuts.

Serve this dish on

whole leaves of crisp lettuce

A happy combination of flavors and textures. To make the chicken even more tender flatten it with the broad side of a meat cleaver before cutting it into slivers.

CHICKEN SEARED WITH GINGER (6)

Clean and chop into 2-inch sections

1 (3-lb.) frying chicken

If the meat is moist, drain the pieces on paper towels. Slice very thin

1 chunk ginger, enough to make about ¼ cup, sliced.

Heat in a large heavy skillet

½ cup oil

When the oil reaches the smoking point, throw in the ginger and chicken. Do not cover the skillet at this point. Maintain high heat and brown the chicken, stirring constantly. Sprinkle it with

½ teaspoon salt
½ teaspoon monosodium glutamate
¼ teaspoon pepper

When the chicken is well browned, reduce the heat and cook for 15 minutes more. Serve only the chicken, discarding the ginger and oil.

The trick in making this dish is to keep all moisture away from the chicken, so that it will absorb the ginger flavor.

CRISPY-SKINNED DUCK (6)

Clean and singe the hairs off

1 (4-5 lb.) duck

Sprinkle the duck liberally with

salt
pepper

Let it stand for an hour or so to permit the salt to penetrate. Meanwhile, devise a steamer which will permit the duck to be steamed without coming into contact with the boiling water. Steam the duck for 3 hours. Cool it, letting any juices drain away while doing so. Truss the duck very securely about the wings and the legs with stout cord.

Fry the duck in

deep fat

until golden brown, turning it by means of the strings. Drain the duck on paper, cut away the strings. Using scissors and a chopping knife, cut the duck into small pieces and arrange them neatly on a large platter.

Garnish the platter with

raw scallions, peeled, cut into 2 inch sections one end of which is cut into strips, like a brush
Suan-mei chiang (Duck Sauce)
Hoi-sin sauce (Chinese barbecue sauce)

Serve the duck with

Sesame seed cakes (page 225)

or

Scallion pancakes (page 226)

The scallions are used to brush the sauces on to the duck.

The rather laborious preparation involved in preparing this dish is offset by its excellence. The meat is tender while the skin is crisp.

LICHEE DUCK (6)

Roast a

4-5 lb. duck

in a 350-375 degree oven for about 2 hours, or until brown and tender. Cool it, propping the duck up so that the fat will drain away from it. Bone the duck and cut it into pieces about 2 inches by 1 inch. Discard the duck fat but strain and save the duck juice.

Measure

1½ cups drained canned lichees
½ cup lichee juice

String

 ¼ lb. snow peas

Heat

 1½ tablespoons oil
 1 teaspoon slivered fresh ginger

Sauté the peas quickly in the oil, removing them from the skillet while they are still jade green. Add to the skillet

 1 tablespoon oil
 ¾ teaspoon salt

Add the duck and the lichee juice. When the duck is heated through, add the lichees and combine the two gently. When these two ingredients are hot, add the snow peas. Mix gently, cook for 1 more minute and serve garnished with

 Chinese parsley

This dish becomes quite simple to prepare if the roast duck is ordered from a store.

DUCK SIMMERED IN BEER (4)

Clean and truss

 1 (5-lb.) duck

Steam the duck for 1 hour, allowing the fat to run off. In a large skillet which will comfortably hold the duck, heat

 3 tablespoons oil

Brown the duck on all sides in the oil. This should take about 10 minutes. At the end of this period add

 2 tablespoons soy sauce

and coat the duck evenly with it. Add

 8 stalks scallions, washed, trimmed and cut into 3 in. sections

Reduce the heat and cover the skillet. Cook the duck for 5 minutes in the soy sauce to permit it to soak into the skin. Now add to the skillet

2 slices fresh orange
½ cup pineapple juice

and coat the duck with

1½ tablespoons plum sauce (suan-mei sauce)

Cover the skillet and cook the duck for about 5 minutes before adding the beer. Simmer the duck in

1½ cups beer

for at least 3 hours, adding more beer as needed. Remove the fat as it comes off. Garnish the duck with a lot of

Chinese parsley

The advantage in this method of cooking is that the gaminess of duck is suppressed while its true flavor is brought out.

MI-FEN, Amoy Style (4)

Soak in hot water for 4 minutes

½ lb. mi-fen (rice noodles)

Drain the noodles in a colander. Shake the colander to rid the noodles of as much moisture as possible.

Prepare

½ lb. pork, cut into slivers
½ lb. shrimp, diced very fine
½ cup soaked Chinese mushrooms, cut into thin slivers
3 stalks scallions, cut into ½ in. sections

Rinse well and drain very thoroughly

½ lb. bean sprouts

In a large skillet heat

3 tablespoons oil

Brown the scallions and add the pork. Sauté it with

2 tablespoons soy sauce.

Add the mushrooms and sauté for 2 minutes. Add the shrimp

to the skillet and sauté them. Maintain high heat. Add the drained bean sprouts and blend all the ingredients. Sauté them until the flavors are brought out, or for about 10 minutes in all. Remove the ingredients from the skillet. Add to the same skillet

2 tablespoons oil

Sauté the drained noodles over high heat for 2-3 minutes or until they have a slightly toasted flavor. Add the pork mixture and cook for 2-3 minutes more, tossing the ingredients lightly with chopsticks and a wooden spoon, as you would a salad. Serve immediately. This style of noodles is usually seasoned with

black pepper
vinegar or hot sauce

Amoy is the name of my hometown. This delicious dish was a specialty of the region, and was commonly sold by street vendors.

FRIED NOODLES

Fry in deep fat until very light brown

transparent noodles, dry

or

rice noodles (mi-fen)

Drain the noodles on absorbent paper.

These crisp noodles may be used to garnish any dish with a creamy texture.

PAOPING (Spring Rolls, Amoy Style) (6)

1. Press as directed on page 173

10 cakes bean curd

Dry the curd with paper towels. Cut it into slivers 1/16 in. broad and 1¼ inches long.

2. Sliver

    1½ lbs. pork tenderloin

3. Drain, discarding the water, and sliver very fine

    2 13 oz. cans bamboo shoots

4. Clean, shell, rinse and dry with paper towels

    1½ lbs. shrimp

Dice it very fine.

5. Wash, drain well and string

    1½ lbs. snow peas

Cut the pods diagonally into very thin slivers.

Sauté the shrimp with

    2 tablespoons oil
    3 stalks scallions cut very fine

Set this aside. Next, sauté the slivered bean curd with

    3 tablespoons oil

Sauté until the slivers are slightly toasted, for about 10 minutes. Remove the curd from the skillet and set it aside. Sauté the pork slivers with

    3 tablespoons oil
    1½ tablespoons soy sauce

Allow about 5 minutes for the pork. Reserve the pork. Sauté the bamboo shoots with

    3 tablespoons oil
    1 teaspoon salt

Cook the shoots for about 5 minutes, stirring constantly. Now combine the pork, the shoots and the bean curd in a very large pot with cover. Heat them over a very slow fire. Stir the ingredients from time to time (approximately every 10 minutes for 1 hour). Then add the shrimp and continue to simmer the mixture over low heat, by stirring for another 30 minutes. Now add the raw slivered snow peas, and cook the ingredients for 45 minutes more, at least, with occasional mixing. The ingredients must be cooked until the flavors of all the ingredients have merged and the pot gives off a superb fragrance. It is a good idea to combine and simmer the ingredients a day ahead and to reheat the mixture over low heat an hour before serving, the total cooking time being at least 2½ hours. Indeed the flavor is improved by letting the mixture stand for a few hours or overnight.

Paoping is served in a large pot which is set in the middle of the table. Around the pot are placed 3 or 4 dishes each of the following ingredients, all of which are served at room temperature.

a. Chiu-ts'ai (a kind of chive obtainable in Chinese grocery stores). Place ½ lb. of the rinsed vegetable in boiling water and parboil it for 3-4 minutes. Cut it into 1-inch sections, discarding the tough ends.

b. 1½-2 cups very finely ground salted peanuts.

c. ½ lb. fresh bean sprouts parboiled for 3 minutes and drained.

d. Egg slivers, made by beating together 6 eggs and ½ teaspoon monosodium glutamate. Make the thinnest possible sheets of egg by placing two tablespoons of egg on a greased skillet and tipping it to make a thin coating. Turn the sheet once. When cool, cut the sheets of egg into thin slivers.

e. Chinese parsley. Break off the tough ends. Wash and drain the parsley. Prepare about 2 cups of the loosely packed leaves.

f. Scallion brushes. Rinse and drain the firm white stalks of 6 scallions. Cut the stalks into 2-in. sections. Slash one end to the height of about ½ in., to make a brush. Arrange the brushes around small dishes of

   Chinese barbecue sauce (Hoi-sin sauce)
   Hot sauce.

Meanwhile, prepare the pancakes in which the filling will be rolled. Allow 4-6 sheets of dough per person. Sift and measure

8 cups flour

Make a well in the middle of the flour and pour into it

approximately 2⅔ cups water

to make a fairly soft dough. Knead and toss the dough briefly on a well floured board. Shape the dough into four long rolls and cut each roll into 7 or 8 equal sections. Shape the dough into a ball between the palms, flatten it on a floured board and roll it with a floured rolling pin into a thin round sheet at least 7 in. in diameter. The circles must not have any holes in them. Grill the dough very lightly on a lightly greased skillet for about 4 minutes on each side, until the sheet acquires a few brown toasted spots, but remains still entirely flexible. Place the cooked sheets on a hot plate and cover it with a hot damp cloth to keep them warm.

To eat paoping, place the dough on a large plate. Each person rolls his own. Place two heaping tablespoonfuls of the filling slightly off center and toward you. Paint the dough with a little barbecue sauce or hot sauce. On top of the filling place teaspoonfuls of parsley, egg slivers, peanuts, etc. according to taste. Make the roll by folding the end nearest you over the filling, then fold the right hand side over the filling to the depth of 1 inch, and then roll the pancake away from you. Naturally, paoping is eaten with the fingers.

Paoping dinners are usually completed with the serving of

Congee (see below)

This dish, or rather, meal, is made about once a year in our home. The combined efforts or two or better still, three people are required and at least one day's work is involved. We usually invite our relatives to make a party of at least six or eight people. It is an Amoy specialty and is really delicious.

CONGEE (6)

Wash

½ cup rice

Bring it to a boil in

1½ quarts water

Simmer the rice for 3-4 hours, until the mixture becomes gruel.

Serve the congee with

Salted duck's eggs, cut in eighths, lengthwise
Preserved eggs, over which a bit of soy sauce and chopped ginger have been sprinkled
Bean cheese, red or white (toufu-ru)
Salted peanuts
Eggs scrambled with fine-chopped dried turnips
Canned Chinese pickles

This menu is included not only because it is good but because it is extremely digestible, a complete change from the rich fare one ordinarily encounters. Note also that it requires little work to prepare.

CURRY PUFFS (about 50 puffs)

Cut

⅔ cup shortening (lard, margarine or butter)

into

2 cups sifted flour

and add to this

⅓ cup ice cold water

Mix this dough lightly, and chill it for twenty minutes. Meanwhile, make the following filling.

Sauté for 5 minutes

1 lb. ground pork

in

1 tablespoon oil or butter

1½ to 2 teaspoons curry

Remove the pork and set it aside to cool.

Sauté in the same skillet

2 large onions cut in rings

adding

1 to 2 tablespoons water

to hasten cooking. When these are tender, mix the onions, pork with

2 tablespoons soy sauce
1 cup cold mashed potatoes

Blend the ingredients thoroughly.

Roll out the chilled dough and cut out circles about 3 inches wide. Place a tablespoon of filling in the center of each circle, double it over and seal the edges, making a scalloped edge. Brush the dough with

a beaten egg yolk

Place the puffs on an ungreased baking sheet, in a 400 degree oven for 25-30 minutes, or until golden brown.

This excellent recipe comes from Mrs. K. Y. Lin. These may be made in advance, cooled after baking and frozen immediately to be reheated in a hot oven as needed. They are very good with cocktails or in a buffet.

SESAME SEED CAKES

Sift together

2 cups flour
½ cup sugar
1½ teaspoons baking powder
¼ teaspoon salt

Blend in

½ cup lard

Add approximately

¼ cup cold water

to make a soft dough. Shape the dough on a floured board into a roll about 1½ inches in diameter. Roll it in wax paper and chill it for 2 hours or more. Cut the dough into ¼ in. rounds. Coat them lightly with

unbeaten egg white

and press the coated side into a mound of

sesame seeds

Place the cakes on an ungreased baking sheet, in a 350 deg. oven for 20 minutes, or until brown. Makes about 2 dozen cakes.

These little cakes are good with fried steamed duck, or they may be served with cocktails.

SCALLION PANCAKES

Sift and measure into a large bowl

5 cups flour

Add to it approximately

1⅔ cups cold water

Stir the mixture with a wooden spoon to make a sticky dough. Flour a board generously. Toss the dough in the flour, kneading it briefly. Keep the board well floured to prevent sticking. Shape the dough into a long roll and cut it into 12 equal parts. With floured hands, roll each piece into a ball. Flour a rolling pin lightly and roll the ball into a circle about 6 inches in diameter.

Make a mixture of

3 tablespoons oil
3 tablespoons sesame seed oil

Prepare

¾ cup chopped scallions

Put a few drops of the oil on top of the circle of dough and spread it evenly with the fingers. Sprinkle the cake generously with salt and with a scant tablespoonful of scallions. Roll up the dough tightly, like a rug, and then roll it up again like a snail curl. Place the snail curl on its side, and with the rolling pin flatten the dough into a circle about 5 in. in diameter. Heat a skillet over a very low flame and barely coat it with oil. A paper towel dipped in some oil and wiped over the skillet will provide the proper amount. Cook the cakes over the lowest possible flame, until light brown spots appear and the dough no longer tastes raw. Each side of the cake will require about 5-6 minutes cooking. Keep the cakes warm until ready to serve. This recipe makes 12 cakes.

These cakes provide an interesting change from the noodles or rice usually served. They are eaten like rolls, that is to say, broken into smaller pieces and eaten with the fingers.

SALTY TWISTS (12 large crullers)

Sift and measure

    3 cups flour

Resift with

    1½ teaspoons salt
    4 teaspoons baking powder

Mix in with a wooden spoon

    1 cup water

Knead the dough on a well-floured board until it is smooth. Form the dough into thin rolls about 3/8 in. wide and 10 inches long. Double it, twist it three or four times, and press down at the ends. Fry the twists in deep fat until golden brown. Drain on absorbent paper. Serve lukewarm or cold, cut into ½ in. sections.

These twists were commonly sold by street vendors in China. Being salty and chewy, they were frequently served at breakfast with congee.

ALMOND PUDDING (6 servings)

Soften

1½ envelopes gelatin

in

½ cup cold water

Scald

1½ cups milk

and dissolve the gelatin in it. When the milk has cooled somewhat, add

2 tablespoons almond extract

Pour the mixture into a large shallow pan. Chill until set. Cut the jelly into diamonds.

Make a syrup of

2 cups water

⅔ cup dark brown sugar

Cool the syrup. Place the cut jelly in a dessert dish and pour over it about ⅓ cup cold syrup.

This simple dessert makes a light ending to an elaborate meal. The jelly may also be served mixed with canned fruit cocktail. In this case, the syrup is omitted and the iced fruit spooned over the jelly.

EIGHT JEWELLED PUDDING

Wash

1¾ cups glutinous rice (nuo-mi)

Add

3½ cups water
4 tablespoons oil

Bring it to a boil, then reduce the heat.

Stir the rice with a wooden spoon. Cook the rice with stirring for 20 to 30 minutes, until it is translucent. Add

1½ cups white sugar

When the sugar is dissolved, remove the rice and cool it.

Choose two deep heatproof bowls with straight sides so that the pudding may be unmolded by inverting it. Grease the bowls with

salad oil

Decorate the pudding with

glazed fruit, cherries and angelica

arranging the pieces upside down at the bottom of each bowl, in a regular pattern. Pack the bottom and sides of the bowl with a 1 in. thick layer of the cooked rice. Place in the center

¾ to 1 cup red bean filling (see below)

or

canned chestnut paste

Cover the filling with 2 inches more of rice, packing it in tightly. Leave a 1 in. space between the pudding and the top of the bowl. Cover the bowl closely with aluminum foil. Place the bowl in boiling water, using a piece of crumpled foil to cushion the bowl. Cover the pot and steam the pudding for 1 hour. The puddings may be removed, cooled and stored in the refrigerator at this point. They will keep very well in this state. Before serving, steam the puddings for another hour and invert them onto plates. Pour over them a hot syrup made with

3 teaspoons cornstarch
1½ cups water
½ cup corn syrup
½ cup sugar

The 2 puddings will serve 12 people.

This festive pudding is usually served at the end of a banquet or a holiday feast. It is rich but delicious. Since it involves quite a lot of work I usually make it in advance and in quantity to be used as needed.

RED BEAN FILLING

Wash

1 cup red beans

and place it in

2½ cups water

Bring to a boil and simmer for about 1½ hours until the beans are very soft. Add to the beans and dissolve

3 tablespoons oil
¾ cup brown or white sugar

Beat the mixture with an electric mixer until a paste is formed. Remove the hulls by forcing the paste through a ricer. The filling may be made in advance and kept frozen.

This filling is available at certain Chinese groceries. It is called tou-sha. *The recipe given here is somewhat less sweet than the store variety.*

RICE DUMPLINGS IN GINGER SOUP
(about 8 servings)

Add sufficient

cold water

to

2 cups glutinous rice flour

to make a dough with the degree of moistness and softness of clay. Pinch off about 1 teaspoonful of the dough at a time, and roll it between the palms to make a ball. Place the balls on waxed paper.

Bring to a boil and simmer for at least 15 minutes

- 7 cups water
- 1 large piece of ginger cut into thin slices
- 2 cups or more of medium or dark brown sugar

When the dumplings are to be cooked, bring the soup to a full boil and drop in the balls gently. Cook the dumplings for about 5 minutes. Serve hot, placing several dumplings in a bowl and ladling the ginger soup over them. This is best eaten using china (not silver) spoons.

This dish is most often encountered at the time of the Chinese New Year. It may be served to visitors at any time of day, and is sufficiently filling to constitute a light meal. The ginger adds zest to the syrup which would otherwise be uninteresting. No special talent is required to make the dumplings which always come out light and downy.

Index